To

Morry and Rose Band, Rabbi Avigdor Miller

To

Bob Kane and Bill Finger, Clayton Moore, Guy Williams,

Robert Stack, Jack Lord, Efrem Zimbalist, Jr., Clint Eastwood,

Adam West, Kyle Chandler

and

To

The real life heroes who selflessly protect and serve,

that we may live safely and securely,

free and confident to live our lives

and pursue our dreams

SPIRITUAL SURVIVAL

FOR

LAW ENFORCEMENT

Spiritual Survival
for
Law Enforcement

Practical Insights, Practical Tools

Rabbi Cary A. Friedman

Foreword by Sergeant Craig Hungler

Spiritual Survival for Law Enforcement
Practical Insights, Practical Tools
by Cary A. Friedman

Published by:
Compass Books
"Books that point the way"
P.O. Box 3091
Linden, NJ 07036
spiritualsurvivalbook.com

Printed in the United States of America

Library of Congress Cataloging-in-Publication Data
Friedman, Cary A.
Spiritual Survival for Law Enforcement:
Practical Insights, Practical Tools
p. cm.
Includes bibliographical references (p.).
ISBN 0976196611
1. Spirituality   2. Law enforcement
3. Psychology / Self-help
Library of Congress Control Number: 2005927201

By the same author

Quis custodiet ipsos custodies?
(Who watches the watchmen?)
– Juvenal, Satires, VI, 347

We ask: Who watches *out for* the watchmen?

* * *

I'm sending out an SOS.
– The *other* Police

CONTENTS

Foreword

STARTING a career in law enforcement is a most exciting time of life. Learning all of the tactical issues and circumstances necessary to stay alive on the streets is an adrenaline rush like no other. We spend hours upon hours training ourselves to be mentally sharp and physically prepared for whatever type encounter we may have during our tour of duty. Departments throughout the country develop physical fitness standards and provide their personnel every opportunity to maintain a high level of physical fitness, realizing the benefit not only to the officer, but agency as well.

In recent years our profession has come a long way in facing emotional issues that we all encounter in a critical incident. The International Critical Incident Stress Foundation has done outstanding work training teams of peers throughout the country to help brother and sister cops return to some level of normalcy when hit with such an incident. The Fraternal Order of Police has taken the lead in forming these peers into C.I.S.M. teams throughout the country and recognizing the great need of ensuring sound emotional and mental health of cops walking that "thin blue line."

Described above are two of the areas that make up a person. Both are required to maintain a whole person. But another area is missing. That missing link is the cop's spiritual being. When thinking of the whole person as made up of three equal parts, physical, mental and spiritual, effort must be given to maintain each arena of life to ensure complete health.

Spirituality is a topic that most cops I know don't spend a lot of time thinking or talking about in their normal daily routine. To think about spirituality leads one at some point to face his or her own mortality, something that we certainly prefer to avoid.

Through this book I hope that you will be able to find something that will spark your interest and passion to build and maintain a healthy spiritual life. There are many avenues in which you are able to build your spiritual life and many people standing alongside of you to assist. I like to think of the analogy of a safety net of faith, or spirituality. When the job is over, either through retirement, resignation, or a critical incident, everything can fall apart in an instant. You need a safety net of a strong faith, to catch you. Without that safety net all can seem hopeless, a feeling that can be fatal. You are too important to feel hopeless.

Many thanks to Rabbi Cary Friedman for pushing this project to conclusion; without his drive and passion I'm not sure it would have made it to print. Thanks as well to the many people who have assisted in the pre-reading and editing of this book, your contribution to the Spiritual health of cops around the world will not be forgotten. Finally, thanks to you, my brothers and sisters who wear the badge throughout this great country. Your service to mankind is indeed a noble calling of God; I pray His blessings of safety upon you and your family.

Sgt. Craig Hungler
Dublin, OH

Spiritual Survival

for

Law Enforcement

I

Why This Book Is Necessary

People tend to think of law enforcement officers as automatons who enforce the law mechanically, emotionlessly, detachedly. Nothing could be further from the truth. A law enforcement officer uses his passion and his compassion – his humanity – in the performance of his duties.

But it is this very sensitivity and concern for those whom he serves – that which we have termed his "humanity" – that makes him susceptible to stresses that are simply unparalleled in any other profession.

A law enforcement officer can better deal with these stresses when he acknowledges his own humanity and the humanity of the community he serves. Ignoring the unique challenges and stresses he faces daily will not make them go away; instead, they will fester and, ultimately, undermine his effectiveness, both professionally and personally, with disastrous consequences.

This book provides a forum for the discussion of these stresses and issues that law enforcement officers face, and offers insights and tools that have the potential to alleviate these stresses.

My hope is that the insights and tools in this book will offer comfort and strength and, in the process, maybe save some careers and even some lives.

Many idealistic young men and women enter the field of law enforcement every year. Their goals are simple yet noble: They wish to "protect and serve," they aspire to protect our society and ensure our welfare. In the pursuit of these lofty goals, they are prepared to risk their very lives.

But who looks out for them? Whose job is it to ensure their well-being?

The story is so familiar and common by now that it is almost a cliché: A bright, idealistic, enthusiastic young officer enters the field; within a few years, there is very little left that resembles the person who graduated the academy. Cynical, dispirited, angry, he is a burned-out husk, a shadow of the person he once was.

And the damage is not limited to the law enforcement officer himself: the officer suffers, and so do the people around him.

Use whatever measure you choose, the overall picture is a grim one. Unhealthy officers develop dangerous attitudes and engage in destructive behaviors, including:

+ alcohol and substance abuse
+ domestic abuse
+ infidelity
+ divorce
+ organic illness
+ rage
+ cynicism
+ depression
+ despair
+ abuse of power
+ professional misconduct
+ suicide *

The downward spiral is predictable and well-documented.

Within the law enforcement community, these problems occur in higher percentages than in the average population. This is problematic enough, but the numbers alone do not correctly communicate the real magnitude of the problem. Consider that the candidates for the academy are subject to the most rigorous screening in order to detect troubled or unstable personalities. The academies take the best of the best – the most stable, balanced, and mentally healthy. By rights, they should succumb to these troubles in far lower percentages than the

---

* Approximately 484 police suicides in 2003, but that number might be much higher. (Robert Douglas, National Police Suicide Foundation)

average population because they are a small, select, elite group. However, the statistics are even worse than that of the average population with its cross section of people, both psychologically healthy and unhealthy. This indicates that something very serious is going on, something far worse than the average population confronts.

Law enforcement is demanding, no question about it. It is difficult for so many reasons. Given its unique challenges, demands, and frustrations, it might not be surprising that so many officers suffer and express that suffering in various destructive and self-destructive ways.

But, clearly, there is another way. This downward spiral is certainly not inevitable. Many officers enjoy long, successful careers. What is the definition of the word "success"? It describes a law enforcement officer who serves honorably, a credit to the badge; maintains his professional enthusiasm; preserves his self-dignity; derives fulfillment from his job; does not succumb to the pressures, escapes, and temptations inherent in the job; does not express frustration violently, whether that violence is directed outwards or inwards; remains at peace with himself; maintains healthy family and social relationships. Those are true measures of success.

What is the difference between the ones who succumb and the ones who survive and even thrive? If all officers are subjected to the same grueling, toxic conditions, what factor accounts for the ones who succeed?

There seem to be a number of factors that contribute to law enforcement officer success. That's what this book is all about.

Numerous books have been written to address (and, perhaps, in the best-case scenario, preempt) the problems encountered by law enforcement officers. With great insight, researchers have realized that the stressors that confront law enforcement officers take many forms. Obviously, some stressors are physical. The physical demands of the job, the danger, shift-work, etc. – these are all physically challenging. But the stressors are not just physical. There is, for example, a hefty emotional component to the stress, as well (*e.g.*, interference with family plans and time together because of shift-work, loss of non-police relationships).

Obviously, to address the physical stressors alone would be inadequate; the emotional stressors would still wreak their havoc and claim their victims. Historically, the law enforcement community ignored the emotional toll that law enforcement takes on its own people. Thank God, that tragic oversight is starting to change. Nowadays, there are training programs and books that address the emotional dimensions of a career in law enforcement.

But there is another component to a career in law enforcement. We often fail to recognize the important, even central, role that spirituality plays in the lives of many, if not most, law enforcement officers. And, therefore, any regimen meant to fortify a law enforcement officer must incorporate a spiritual dimension as well, else it will be incomplete and fail to achieve its goal.

This book is an attempt to address that spiritual dimension.

It is unfortunate that insights into spirituality and spiritual survival like the ones described in this book were not available for earlier generations as a standard feature of every academy curriculum. Many officers already knew about them or intuited them; but many did not. And many suffered as a result of their lack of awareness.

At the end of roll call, the sergeant on "Hill Street Blues," Sgt. Phil Esterhaus, used to say, "Let's be careful out there." It's good advice. To which I would add: "... and *in here*, inside you, where perhaps an even greater danger lurks."

"SPIRITUAL HEALTH" AND "EMOTIONAL HEALTH"

We must distinguish between spiritual health and emotional health. While the two share some characteristics, there are also many differences.

Spiritual stress is similar to emotional stress in that the scars it produces are not physically apparent, but they exist, nevertheless, and they can hurt very badly – and left untreated, they can kill.

Still, spiritual health is a separate dimension of a human being and a need in its own right.

Emotional health is essentially internally directed. Emotional health involves ensuring that one has the ability to process and work through experiences and stimuli. Some police experiences – crime scenes or accident scenes, for example – can be emotionally draining or overwhelming. Emotional health refers to one's ability to recover from those experiences and stimuli in order to be able to respond later in other situations in an appropriate manner. Emotional health refers to one's ability to handle the emotional baggage that one picks up in the course of doing the job. Emotional health prevents one from being trapped, helplessly, in dark emotional states.

By contrast, spiritual health means to step outside of oneself and connect with something external to, and higher than, oneself. It is letting in something from without. It involves acting and looking at oneself from the vantage point of higher, absolute values. Those values could be religious, but they don't need to be. Spiritual health describes how a person responds to, and behaves based on, these external considerations. It's about the reasons and considerations that go into the decisions a person makes. When we think about spiritual health, we need to consider something – some source of inspiration or motivation – outside the person. Picture a compass and magnetic true north: the compass is the person, and true north is the source of values that inspires and motivates the person to act the way he does.

Thus, while emotional health is primarily concerned with a person's internal sense of wholeness, spiritual health is concerned with how a person interacts with an external value system.

Indeed, for many law enforcement officers, it is the spiritual side that prompted them to enter the field in the first place, and it is the spiritual side – that reservoir of energy and inspiration – that keeps them healthy in the field.

If emotional health were the only consideration, most law enforcement officers would probably leave the field. A career in law enforcement is a pretty big threat to emotional health, and requires constant, active efforts to restore emotional health. In contrast, it is the dimension of the spirit that motivates a person to go into, and remain in, the field of law enforcement.

Think of it this way: When you own a car, you need to maintain the engine in good working order and you need to supply that engine with fuel to run it. The emotional dimension may keep your engine healthy and functioning properly, but the spiritual dimension provides the fuel – high octane fuel – that runs the engine and directs it to accomplish amazing things.

It is an interesting fact that one might be emotionally healthy (in that one can process the experiences of law enforcement) but nevertheless reach a state of being spiritually unhealthy where one is tempted to harm – even kill – oneself. We will consider this state later in this discussion. Suffice to say right now that emotional health is *not* enough to ensure success in law enforcement. Even one who has acquired the tools for dealing with the emotional challenges of the career may become disillusioned and spiritually ill by what he encounters daily on the job, with severe consequences.

A law enforcement officer dares not settle for anything less than physical, emotional, and spiritual health. Each component is absolutely essential to success in the field.

"WHY IS *MY* SPIRITUAL WELL-BEING ANYONE'S BUSINESS BUT MY OWN?"

It is completely understandable why an officer should be concerned about his own spiritual well-being. After all, he's got a lot at stake – his professional career and personal life. But you hear a lot of talk nowadays about a new-found concern by law enforcement agencies and departments for the spiritual health of law enforcement officers. Why should this be a source of concern for any agency or for the law enforcement community in general? Why is it anyone's business, other than that of the law enforcement officer himself?

There are many reasons to care about the spiritual health of each and every law enforcement officer:

(1) Kept in good working order, a law enforcement officer can provide several decades of good police work. Obviously, it is worth it to invest whatever effort is needed to maximize the payoff of the initial investment of sending him to the academy. From a dollars and cents perspective, it makes sense to keep our officer in good working order.

On the other hand, if he isn't healthy, we can lose him from police work. Officers who succumb to the stressors of the job can irreparably harm their careers in many ways and render themselves unable to continue in police work. In the most extreme case, the law enforcement officer can hurt himself (or even others) physically.

(2) If the law enforcement officer is spiritually unhealthy and continues in the job, the results can be even more disastrous than if we were to lose him entirely from the career. If a law enforcement officer is unhealthy, then the *entire* community is in danger. An unhealthy officer can create a whole world of problems. He can:

+ create a serious rift between the police and the public
+ irreparably tarnish the image of the police through abuse of power
+ undermine the authority, prestige, and credibility of the police
+ inspire fear and mistrust amongst the citizenry, and polarize the public and police.

A spiritually healthy law enforcement officer is just about the best resource a community can have. Thus, whether the agency's concern is the well-being of the individual law enforcement officer or the well-being of the community, the strategies to ensure well-being converge in ensuring the spiritual health of each and every law enforcement officer.

Who Are the Officers *Most* at Risk for Spiritual Unhealth?

Dr. Kevin Gilmartin, in his wonderful book, *Emotional Survival for Law Enforcement*, observes a tragic irony in the realm of emotional *un*health: The officers who are most at risk for emotional unhealth are those who start out the most enthusiastic to do the job right. Their enthusiasm and resolve to be the very best officers they can be leaves them especially vulnerable to the emotional dangers of law enforcement. Ironically, officers who enter the field halfheartedly or disinterestedly, who perform their job lackadaisically, don't face the same potentially high emotional risks that Dr. Gilmartin describes. (These mediocre officers face their own unique challenges that make them, ultimately, unsuitable for, and unsuccessful in, the job of law enforcement; but that's another discussion.)

This same tragic irony exists in the spiritual realm: The officers most at risk for spiritual unhealth are those who are the most conscientious, who throw themselves into the job, who have the most integrity, who start out as the most idealistic, who feel deeply and care sincerely, but who might not have a strong spiritual basis to support or replenish their idealism and commitment. They are the ones most at risk for spiritual disillusionment and profound spiritual unhealth. Ironically, officers who enter the field and perform their job halfheartedly, disinterestedly, without investment of heart and soul, don't face the same potential high spiritual risks described in this book. (Here, too, this is not meant to imply that the disinterested ones make better officers. Far from it. These mediocre officers suffer from their own unique challenges that make them, ultimately, unsuitable for, and unsuccessful in, the job of law enforcement, but that, too, is for another time.)

The greater the investment and the more one opens oneself up to do the job well, the greater the potential for depth of pain, loss of faith, and loss of hope.

On the other hand, these conscientious, deeply idealistic

officers are also the ones with the most openness to spiritual values and who have the greatest capacity to reach spiritual greatness in their own development as human beings.

Most officers enter passionately and idealistically. They are at greater risk for spiritual disillusionment, but also possess greater capacity to reach spiritual greatness. I hope to show you how to use the experiences of a law enforcement career to reach great spiritual heights.

THIS BOOK IS DESIGNED FOR BOTH THE ROOKIE COP AND THE SEASONED OFFICER

In fact, this book is useful in three ways:

(1) A couple of years out in the field, most officers "hit a wall": They undergo a profound change in their outlooks, they experience a crisis. They find themselves disillusioned by the career; they wonder where that high-mindedness with which they entered the field has gone. Very often this includes confronting what seems like a gigantic mountain of challenges to the beliefs they held when they entered the career. They feel vaguely betrayed. They feel burned out. Where once there was clarity and resolution, now there is doubt and unhappiness. It's an empty, lonely, lousy feeling.

The spiritual insights we present have much to offer to counter that anger, anxiety, depression, and disillusionment.

(2) If you are just entering the field of law enforcement, some of this – perhaps all of it – might not make too much sense to you. Sadly, one day it probably – inevitably – will. Master these skills now so that, when you need them, you will be familiar with the ideas and expert in the use of these tools. My real goal, though, is to help you preempt as much as possible these potential problems and ensure that you'll never have that moment of searing pain and turmoil. That is certainly my hope and prayer.

It is a little late to wait until an officer is out in the field to first introduce ideas about spirituality and the consolation and healing power spirituality can bring. It is far better, and much more effective, to introduce these insights at the academy stage, long before an officer has reached the breaking point. These ideas might not make a lot of sense then, but they will later on, when the officer encounters a crisis.

(3) Even in the absence of a crisis, these insights have much to offer a law enforcement officer.

Think of physical health for a moment. Even if one is not sick, that is still a far cry from being truly healthy and feeling the robustness of good health with its vigor, energy, and enthusiasm.

The same is true for spiritual health. Healthy spirituality can contribute significantly to emotional well-being, job satisfaction, self-esteem, inner peace, and a sense of purpose.

"SPIRITUALITY" DOES *NOT* EQUAL "RELIGION"

Spirituality is not the same as religion.

Spirituality is a broad topic, of which religion is a subset. Spirituality is about the human spirit, and religion – every religion – is but a means of expressing that human spirit, and but one particular expression of the human spirit.

"Religion is the manner in which an individual lives out his/her spirituality, usually in some type of formal structure, institution, or organization. Spirituality is, therefore, broader than religion. Spirituality can be described as one's relationship with three realities: (1) a transcendent higher being (which some choose to call God), (2) one's self, and (3) the universe, including other individuals. ... Spirituality is the means whereby human beings relate to these realities and entities." (*Suicide and Law Enforcement*, page 508)

If you are, or choose to be, religious, that's great. Religion can be a fine expression of the human spirit and its yearnings. But you don't necessarily have to be religious in order to reap the benefits that spiritual insights and tools offer.

These spiritual insights can enhance, or serve as a very

effective, powerful complement to an already rich religious life.

USING THIS BOOK

You don't need to be religious to use this book and its insights to advantage. It's true that we discuss some basic theology occasionally (mostly in chapter 2), and even invoke God once in a while.

But even if you don't believe in God in the conventional religious sense, nevertheless, this book will speak to you and inspire you if the world of the spirit is important to you. In place of "God," use whatever source of transcendent truth and inspiration moves you. Substitute it with the source that defines for you some larger absolute value system of morality, compassion, concern, responsibility, truth, justice, and mercy. For many, that Source is God. Perhaps you have another.

The masculine form is used throughout this book to refer to the law enforcement officer, even though some of the finest officers in the field are women. No slight is intended.

This book should also give you a sense of what a good, competent chaplain should be doing. Use it to find yourself a good chaplain who will support your efforts to create and maintain spiritual health. Use it also to lose a bad one who would, unwittingly, undermine your efforts towards spiritual health.

Use this book as a springboard for discussion with your colleagues in the context of a group discussion. Think of it as the traditional "choir practice," minus alcohol and mental disease. Elaborate on a point, and offer anecdotes from your own life experience. Sometimes it's easier to discuss a problem or issue when you can discuss it in the third person ("I have this friend in the Valley/ninth precinct ...," "It says in this book ...," "Can you believe this guy? He claims ...," etc.) Disagree violently with my observations and points – that's OK, too: Discuss that with your colleagues, too, and define your own particular set of beliefs.

Use it to clarify for yourself your own unique reasons for

doing the job you do.

How to Get the Most Out of This Book

Obviously, the benefit from a book such as this comes not from reading it once, but from rereading it time and again. Review this book frequently and revisit its ideas to fortify yourself. Discussion groups or periodic debriefings based upon the ideas presented here can be very helpful.

What This Book Is *Not*

Please remember that this book is not a pitch or an excuse or a license to use your sacred position as law enforcement officer to proselytize or in any way shove your religious views down other people's throats. It is highly inappropriate and unethical to force any religious doctrine or belief on any officer, crime victim, or any other person. The tools and insights that we will present are meant to give you inner strength and nourishment; they are not meant to be a weapon with which to bludgeon other people over the head.

In large part, these insights are meant to serve as background music as you do what you do in the course of your day, to help you appreciate with greater clarity the greatness of what you do and its transcendent value and cosmic significance. You might find some like-minded law enforcement officers with whom to discuss these ideas – hence my suggestions for exercises to be done in groups.

A group of law enforcement officers who share your views is a wonderful resource. But no one should be forced to be an unwilling participant or audience in religious or spiritual dialogue or be forcibly exposed to your heavy-handed force-feeding of religious beliefs. You might think you are being subtle or clever in getting your ideas in "under the wire" – you're not. To force your religious beliefs upon other people is an abuse of your office and power; you betray the very ideas you claim to espouse and have promised to protect. And, ironically, you rob those ideas of their power to inspire and nourish.

Better to let others see the benefits of such belief in your exemplary behavior. In the long run, nothing is more compelling than the image of a person of faith who behaves consistently in accordance with all those ideas he claims to believe.

A Note to Clergy

Ministry to law enforcement officers requires special education, training, and sensitivity to enable a chaplain to provide the appropriate spiritual nourishment that is such an integral part of total health and restoration for a law enforcement officer. A good law enforcement chaplain needs to become familiar with the effects of anger, fear, confusion, and faith crises experienced by those who encounter crime, evil, and tragedy so closely and intimately. This book can be a good beginning text, a first look into the spiritual world of the law enforcement officer.

A clergy person should not make the mistake of thinking that ministry to law enforcement officers is just an extension of ministry to civilians and parishioners. It's a different kind of work, and it requires specialized training and insights. Without the benefit of that training and insight, even a very good, effective minister can be a very bad, ineffective or downright destructive chaplain.

Who Should Read This Book?

If you're a law enforcement officer, you should read this book, *and so should your loved ones*. Give it to your family (including wife or husband, kids, parents, sisters and brothers) and significant others to read, so they can understand you better and work together with you in creating health.

Give it to your pastor – minister, priest, rabbi, imam, shaman, you name it – to read. They might never have received formal training in ministering to law enforcement officers and they might have no idea about the unique realities confronting law enforcement officers. This might inspire them to learn how to minister to law enforcement officers. Tell them for us: There is no nobler ministry a pastor can provide.

"I GET BY WITH A LITTLE HELP FROM MY FRIENDS": IMAGES EVOKED IN THIS BOOK

In the course of this discussion, I have at times tried to lighten up what is a pretty heavy topic by invoking the images of famous iconic pop-culture fictional policemen and detectives from TV, movies, and literature. It is certainly not meant to trivialize the ideas; instead, my goal is to keep the reader's attention and interest and encourage him to use his imagination to understand the particular point under discussion on a deep, visceral, gut level.

Don't be fooled by the lighthearted tone that is sometimes used. This is not a fluffy discussion by any means. The underlying ideas are quite profound, very powerful, and extremely helpful.

People can't get enough of fictional law enforcement officers. Why? Because they demonstrate that chaos and evil need not win – that good can triumph over evil as long as there are people who are noble and brave enough to be willing to stand up and fight for the good. They produce order out of what would otherwise be chaos, and people fear chaos. They demonstrate resolve and courage and the willingness to confront, battle, and vanquish evil.

You demonstrate that also, every day of your professional life, no matter how much people grumble because you just gave them that ticket. In their heart of hearts they know what you are and do, and they are grateful for it. It's a little harder to identify the real-life person (who gives the tickets and all that) with that image of justice; it is much easier to identify justice in the screen image of the law enforcement officer. But it's all there just the same, and they sense it in you nevertheless.

THE NEED TO FORTIFY ONESELF SPIRITUALLY

Success in a career in law enforcement depends upon the strength, intensity, and clarity of the law enforcement officer's spiritual values that motivated him to enter the field and motivate him to remain in the field. A law enforcement officer cannot survive the unique, extreme rigors of the field and enjoy a long, productive, satisfying career without vigorous, robust, compelling, powerful motivation.

The unique challenges and stresses of a career in law enforcement have the potential to "dispirit" the officer. When an officer becomes dispirited, he loses confidence in his, or anyone's, ability to effect real, meaningful change in this evil, corrupt world; he loses faith – in himself, in other people, in God; he loses hope – that is, he loses the ability to envision a better world. When that grim, evil reality he confronts becomes the only reality that he knows, can envision or foresee, then all too often the "dispirited" officer becomes a danger to himself and the people around him. We have all heard the tragic statistics regarding officer suicide, marital conflict, promiscuity, illness, etc.

Aerobic exercise, psychological counseling, and other strategies are all important and helpful, and have their unique place in the regimen of strengthening the law enforcement officer. But the challenges threatening the officer are essentially spiritual in nature. It is a challenge that must be responded to in kind. Since the threat is spiritual in nature, its antidote must also be spiritual: the fortification of the spirit of the officer.

Stress management is very important, and must be taught early in one's career; but it cannot be a substitute for the vital and indispensable job of fortifying the spirit of the officer.

Each challenge makes a demand upon, draws from, the officer's spiritual reserves; those reserves must be replenished, and we must provide an officer with the means to replenish them.

The Need to "Protect and Serve" Yourself

You took an oath to "protect and serve." It is a strange, tragic irony that the one citizen out there in your world who does not enjoy the benefit of your protection and service is *you*.

If my appeals to care for yourself *for your sake* fall on deaf ears, I'll try it another way: You want to be the best cop you can be, right? The only way to do that is by taking care of yourself. There just isn't any other way. So care for yourself *for their* (*i.e.*, the community you serve's) *sake*.

It is a fact of human nature that a person's ability to empathize with, and look benevolently at, the rest of the world depends upon how much empathy and benevolence he demonstrates for himself. If you neglect yourself and allow yourself to languish, unattended, you will not be able to feel concern for others – but that's exactly why you entered this career in the first place, in order to feel concern for, and help, other people.

"The remarkable thing is that we really do love others as ourselves. We hate others when we hate ourselves. We love others when we love ourselves. It is not love of self but rather hatred of self that is at the root of mankind's problems." (Eric Hoffer, *The Passionate State of Mind*, # 100)

You have to love and care for yourself in order to do your job properly. The care and feeding of *you* is the indispensable prerequisite for you to be able to function effectively – compassionately and empathetically – as a law enforcement officer.

You came into a career in law enforcement upbeat, passionate, idealistic (!), and very inspired. Our goal is to help keep you that way.

II

THE WORLD OF THE SPIRIT

SOME BASIC, "DOWN TO EARTH" THEOLOGY

In this chapter, I'm going to present a basic religious perspective on life and law enforcement. An appreciation of a religious perspective might further deepen and enhance your appreciation of the material in later chapters.

I will present a coherent spiritual perspective of life, this world, and what we human beings are doing in it. If you've ever wondered where you "fit in" in the cosmic scheme of things, so to speak, in this chapter we will locate you on the spiritual map with a big "X," a kind of "you are here" on the map of Creation. It is not my intent to root the discussion in any particular religion. My goal, instead, is to introduce a kind of "no frills," generic religious perspective.

While this chapter is phrased in religious language, its true goal is to foster awareness, clarity, and comfort. Feel free to use it as a template for developing your own philosophy. At some point, for the sake of spiritual health on the job, you should define what you know to be true and what you think is true. Law enforcement is not a neutral career when it comes to spiritual issues; it's not a purely technical kind of job like, say, plumbing. It demands some thoughts and decisions and definite opinions about spirituality – that is, if you plan to survive a long career of law enforcement.

✦ Because law enforcement is so intensely challenging spiritually, because law enforcement makes so many demands on you spiritually, you can't just ignore the world of the spirit and never give it any thought. You simply don't have that luxury. It's essential to know what you know, think, and believe about the world of the spirit.

WHY WE'RE HERE:
THE PURPOSE OF LIFE

God, the Creator, created the universe and all that is within it. He created every human being and endowed him with an animating spark of Divinity, the human soul. As a result of this spark, every human life is infinitely valuable and precious in potential, and every human being possesses an endless capacity and potential for accomplishment.

We exist in This World for a purpose, to prepare for the Next World by refining our souls. Each of us is given a "raw" soul, and our job is to mold, refine, and elevate it in anticipation of returning it to the Creator in the Next World. Everything we do here is a preparation for the eternal existence we will experience in the World to Come.

That doesn't trivialize our existence here in This World. On the contrary, it enhances it, invests it – every second of it – with tremendous meaning and importance. Our actions are significant, and God is aware of and cares about everything every human being does.

In creating the universe, God left room for each human being to be a partner with Him in the perfection of that world. God taught humankind certain fundamental rules governing human behavior and interaction – it is wrong to steal or murder, for example – so that one human being not hurt the person or property of another human being. God taught humanity the virtues of kindness, justice, truth, peace, mercy. God charged every human being with a mission: to protect His world and His children, of which every human being is one.

We are to perfect the world – physically and socially – by adhering to and practicing these transcendent Godly values. God expects us to choose the good and reject the evil. When evil and tragedy threaten the world, through natural or human agents, we are enjoined to battle those wherever they appear.

FREE WILL

Of all the creatures God created, we are unique in that we

humans alone – in contradistinction to everything else in the universe except God – possess free will. We share this feature with God and no one else. The heavenly beings do not possess free will. They perform God's will perfectly, without failing, because they cannot help but perform His bidding. Animals behave according to innate instincts – they do not choose to do good or evil. Not so a human being. We are not compelled to behave in a particular way. We possess free will, the ability to decide how to behave. This is what it means to be created in the "image of God." God exhorts us: "I have placed before you today life and good, and death and evil, … blessing and curse, and you shall *choose* life" (*Deuteronomy* 30:19).

Every person's actions are significant. A human is given the free will to decide how he will use that awesome power, that infinite capability, with which God endowed him. Actions have repercussions and each person must take the responsibility for his own actions. Eventually, every person will be required to give an accounting of his actions before God.

Of course, no person ever behaves perfectly all the time. We all make mistakes. That is the result of having free will. But our service to Him, our pursuit of the good in this world, is valuable because of our freedom of choice.

There are many people out there who try hard to pursue the good. They may fail occasionally, but they are heading in the right direction, and it is precisely this process which is so precious to God.

The flip side of providing humanity with free will is that some people will choose to embrace evil. When you see people who are thoroughly wicked, know that they are misusing the free will with which they were endowed. Know, too, that other people have not misused their gift of free will.

That's the pesky problem with free will. People have to be able to exercise it. What value is there in good behavior when the person has no other option? Answer: It is meaningless. The active choice of good is only noble and noteworthy when the possibility exists to choose evil.

The wicked of this world serve an important function: They provide the resistance against which we struggle and strive in order to refine and elevate ourselves. The battle against evil is the motivation that ennobles us, that demands that we reach inward and find a will and the resolve to struggle against evil and injustice. If there were no such challenges, we might never turn inward and find that resolve, strength of will, and character needed to fight evil – and we would never become spiritually great in the process.

It is, perhaps, a troubling truth that we do not turn inward and find the greatness within ourselves until we must confront the basest wickedness of other people. Faced with no challenge, people can become lazy and complacent. When danger – and the greatest danger is the myriad expressions of human evil and wickedness – threatens, people turn inward and tap into unbelievable reservoirs of strength, resolve, conviction, and decency. If a law enforcement officer's career introduces him to the depths of depravity that people can sink to when they exercise free will to choose evil, his career also introduces and ushers him to the heights of nobility to which people can rise when they exercise their free will to choose good.

Some people are a little of both, perhaps driven by no strong feelings on either side. They may know intellectually that they should do good, but their emotions or desires or passions may overpower their intellects. Not so the law enforcement officer. Given the nature of the job he performs, the law enforcement officer doesn't have this option of remaining neutral.

THE RELIGIOUS SIGNIFICANCE
OF LAW ENFORCEMENT

A law enforcement officer protects God's world and His children. He is a partner – nothing less – with God in the perfection of that God-created world. He protects the legal structure that ensures the safety of person and property of every citizen. In doing this, he acknowledges the humanity and dignity – the

Divine spark – of every citizen. When evil and tragedy threaten, he battles against them and serves as a symbol for everyone else. He is a symbol that Good has the will to battle, and the ability to triumph over, Evil. He is the order that will confront and vanquish chaos. He is the exemplar of all those Godly virtues of kindness, justice, truth, peace, mercy.

A law enforcement officer actively chooses to "do good" every time he puts on the badge. He accomplishes this in several different ways:

+ He thwarts the bad guys, the ones who chose to do evil: He prevents them from realizing their schemes.

+ He protects the good guys, and enables them to live their lives and pursue their destinies free from concern for predators.

+ He serves as the human manifestation in this world of fear of God that motivates people – strongly! – to behave.

The laws of this country are drawn from, and approximate, the Law, and adherence to the law will allow a person to come pretty darn close to obeying God's will. Intellectual consideration of the theoretical specter of punishment in the Next World may not be sufficient to deter one from misbehaving, but the prospect of silent alarms, flashing red lights, handcuffs, a stint in jail – all tangible, concrete images – may just do it. The officer's presence in the equation encourages many people to choose to be good because misbehavior brings with it too many negative consequences.

A law enforcement officer exercises his freedom of will to do good every time he battles wickedness or injustice, upholds the law, and protects the weak and oppressed. Each time he confronts and thwarts misbehavior or punishes lawbreakers, he must turn inward and pull out greater and greater amounts of selflessness, devotion to the law, etc. The difficulty of the battle forces him to turn inward and find a greatness of character he possessed in potential before – but now it is actualized.

People are not perfect, but they are not intrinsically incorrigible, either. No person is forced to be good or evil. And even an imperfect person can accomplish tremendous amounts of good in this world and earn God's approval.

Man's task in the world … is to transform fate into destiny; a passive existence into an active existence; an existence of compulsion, perplexity, and muteness into an existence replete with a powerful will with resourcefulness, daring, and imagination. We ask neither about the cause of evil nor about its purpose but rather about how it might be mended and elevated. How shall a person act in a time of trouble? What ought a man to do so that he not perish in his afflictions? The … answer to this question is very simple. Afflictions come to elevate a person to purify and sanctify his spirit, to cleanse and purge it of the dross of superficiality and vulgarity, to refine his soul and to broaden his horizons. The … sufferer commits a grave sin if he allows his troubles to go to waste and remain without meaning or purpose.

– *Rabbi Joseph Soloveitchik*

That is the religious significance, and real job description, of law enforcement.

WHY DON'T MORE PEOPLE RECOGNIZE THIS?

It is a curious feature of spiritually significant activities that those who perform them often do so without the benefit of the public's acclaim and accolades. Perhaps God designed the world in this way to test or guarantee the sincerity of the person performing those spiritually significant activities. Every law enforcement officer, frequently subjected to distrust or even vilification by the same public he serves and protects, can attest to the existence of this curious phenomenon.

THE IMMORTALITY OF THE HUMAN SOUL, REWARD AND PUNISHMENT

The human soul is eternal. When a person dies physically in This World, the immortal soul – the essence of the person – does not die. Rather, it transitions to the Next World, there to be compensated in accordance with its behavior in This World. In that Next World, injustices in This World are rectified. God is the Divine Judge, and He ensures that no one escapes the consequences of his behavior, for good or bad. This concept of reward and punishment is fundamental to a conception of a Just God Who is interested in humanity, and the Next World is often the place where the cosmic accounts are balanced.

Part of the reward or punishment of the Next World is an awareness of the consequences of our actions in This World, and we are shown what processes we set into motion through our behavior. Thus God, Who alone can discern the effects our individual actions have on all of Creation, shows each person how each and every action ripples throughout Creation and history. Watching the wide-ranging – indeed, cosmic – beneficial effect of a good deed is obviously very pleasurable; and watching the wide-ranging – indeed, cosmic – destructive harm of each bad deed is obviously very embarrassing and painful. Pleasure or pain that we will ultimately experience is a part of what is sometimes referred to as "Heaven" or "Hell."

THE ULTIMATE SACRIFICE IS THE ULTIMATE INVESTMENT

One can make observations from the vantage point of religion or spirituality that one cannot make from an observation point down here on earth.

From this religious/spiritual vantage point comes the observation that *sacrifice is not an end – it's an investment*. An officer who gives his life in the line of duty presents his soul back to the Almighty in the Next World and declares, "I was willing to give all that I had to protect Your children, to defend the values of justice and morality. It wasn't just idle talk."

Our job in This World is to refine our characters and elevate our souls through the performance of good deeds and to care for His children, in preparation for returning that refined, elevated soul to God in the Next World. The officer who cherished the concepts of justice, service, and protection such that he gave his life has not reached an end by any means. Rather, he has made an investment, which will pay tremendous dividends for an eternity in the Next World.

That said, it is an investment we are committed to preventing. We would rather that you return your refined, elevated soul to the Creator after a long, successful, happy career and life characterized by that kind of nobility. And so would God.

THE "CIVIC RELIGION" OF THE UNITED STATES OF AMERICA

This conception of God and His plans for humanity that I have presented in this chapter is consistent with the conception of God conjured up by the sacred, defining documents (such as the Constitution) of the United States of America and the "American civic religion" defined by those documents. This is the God before Whom an officer takes his officer's oath. This is God, in Whose presence a witness in a court of law swears to tell the truth. This is God, Whom we acknowledge before opening every session of Congress or the Supreme Court. This is God, Whose blessing we seek when we say "God bless America." This is God, in Whom we trust.

THE RELIGIOUS SIGNIFICANCE OF THE AMERICAN LEGAL SYSTEM

One of God's commandments for humanity contained in

the "Seven Noachide Commandments"* is to set up and maintain a just, equitable system of laws to govern society.

No human law is perfect, of course, but the legal system of the United States of America, with its Constitution and Bill of Rights, is a system second to none. The Founding Fathers created a legal system that would produce a society of freedom, equality, and justice, and that system continues to evolve to a more perfect system. As such, it satisfies the definition of a decent system of human law, in accordance with the Noachide Code for humanity.

We can be proud of our legal system. When we consider the system the Founding Fathers created, the free society it has produced, the liberties it has safeguarded, we can have no doubt but that its creators, the Founding Fathers, who were themselves devout believers and who approached their work in a spirit of divine service, were given divine assistance in reaching their goals and creating this country.

Upholding that legal system and the integrity of the law is also a fulfillment of that Noachide commandment to set up and maintain a just, equitable system of laws.

Law enforcement officers are the priests of the secular religion ("law") even as clergy are the priests of the ecclesiastical religion ("Law"). One group is in law enforcement; the other, in Law enforcement. And the two concepts, law and Law, are – historically and philosophically – inextricably wrapped up in each other.

---

* The Seven Noachide Commandments are:
  1. Believe in God's Unity: *Do not worship idols*
  2. Respect and Praise God: *Do not blaspheme*
  3. Respect Human Life: *Do not murder*
  4. Respect Family: *Do not have forbidden relations*
  5. Respect the Rights of Others: *Do not steal*
  6. Respect All Creatures: *Do not eat flesh taken from a live animal*
  7. Pursue Justice: *Set up courts to uphold laws*

III

THE SPIRITUAL DIMENSION
OF LAW ENFORCEMENT

YOU'RE familiar, of course, with what you do on a daily basis.

Let's revisit those things you do and see them again, aware, this time, of their true nature and significance.

A LAW ENFORCEMENT OFFICER IS A SPIRITUAL BEING

Why does someone enter the field of law enforcement? Has he not read the dissuasive statistics, heard the disheartening anecdotes? There are dangers – physical, emotional, social, and familial. Doesn't he know all this? And if he does know, why would he expose himself to these dangers? Why does he enter the field?

Is it the desire for money? Glory? Power? If it is any of these, then he is doomed to failure in his career. Those motivations will not nourish, protect, or inspire an officer for very long.

Most officers – the good ones, anyway – enter law enforcement because they want "to protect and serve." They enter because they want to bestow good upon others. They enter because there is tragedy and evil and chaos in the world – lurking behind every corner, it seems – and left unchecked it has the potential to sweep away and engulf all that exists. Someone has to protect all those innocent people – civilians – who would otherwise be vulnerable, helpless, and dispirited in the face of all that tragedy.

Consider the typical recruit who enters the field of law enforcement. He enters the academy with a powerful desire "to protect and serve." This enthusiastic desire to serve, even at the risk of his own safety, is driven by a profoundly idealistic ambition.

> All that is necessary for the triumph of evil
> is for good men to do nothing.
> – *Edmund Burke*

+ Chaos
+ indifference
+ irresponsibility
+ selfishness
+ fear
+ and evil

all threaten our society, so the law enforcement officer ...

+ imposes order
+ demonstrates concern
+ assumes responsibility
+ practices selflessness and self-sacrifice
+ shows resolve and confidence to battle
+ and champions justice.

All those corrosive, toxic dangers the law enforcement officer is exposed to: Had it not been for him, *we* would have been exposed to them. He buffers the citizenry – potential victims all – from them; his actions detox them for the public. But he receives a full, undiluted dose of all those toxins.

The law enforcement officer is the antidote for us. The law enforcement officer represents the best of human resolve, will, sacrifice, strength, justice, and courage – all that is most nobly human, most genuinely spiritual. He *inspires* the community he serves. It is significant that the word "inspire" is derived from the word "spirit" – *i.e.*, the law enforcement officer infuses us with a measure of his own noble spirit, and we partake of his spiritual strength.

Where once we might have been overwhelmed, paralyzed by fear, cowed by malevolence, and disillusioned, instead – *because of the law enforcement officer* – we are comforted, inspired and strengthened. If we civilians do not lose our faith, in God or in humans, it is in large part because of the law enforcement officer.

It is a striking phenomenon that there are families that are filled with law enforcement officers and members of the clergy. They enter these fields interchangeably because they recognize that both careers provide opportunities for ministering to, and inspiring, the human beings around us. Often, law enforcement officers will confide, "I was debating between a career in the clergy and in law enforcement, and decided to go into law enforcement. But my grandfather(s)/uncle(s)/brother(s) is/are ministers, and my grandfather(s)/uncle(s)/brother(s) is/are cops." In many ways, it seems, the careers are interchangeable.

Similarly, it is not an accident that law enforcement officers and clergy just naturally seem to get along. There is a natural affinity and a strong bond because, in essence, they are remarkably alike. The parallels between the ministries of clergy and law enforcement are uncanny. They include:

✦ Ministering
✦ Protecting
✦ Serving
✦ Setting examples
✦ Enforcing laws
✦ Answering to a higher authority

What a job description! Is that a heavy burden? It certainly is. That shield, although it weighs only a few ounces, can weigh very heavily on an officer.

Did the law enforcement officer aspire to this when he entered the job? For most law enforcement officers, the answer seems to be yes. Their reasons for entering the career are noble and spiritual.

Some, aware of their own very spiritual stirrings, do indeed express themselves quite explicitly, eloquently, and inspirationally in this way. Those self-aware officers are in pretty good shape, spiritually equipped to face the challenges the career will throw at them. If that, indeed, is your motivation for doing the job *and you know it*, then you are already well on your way to enjoying a measure of spiritual protection and vitality that can protect you through a long career in law enforcement.

Some are a little less aware. They might not articulate those aspirations and motivations in such spiritual terminology and with such clarity, but they do express, using more basic and intuitive terminology, many of the same sentiments.

Many, unfortunately, are not really consciously aware of this whole dimension of their decision. And that can cause problems down the line.

LAW ENFORCEMENT IS SPIRITUAL WORK

Having spiritual values and motivations is not unique to the law enforcement profession or officer, of course. Most people, if asked, would profess to having deeply held spiritual values. Asked about the strength of their convictions, people will often say that, given the need, they would die for them. And, indeed, perhaps they would.

But people are rarely called upon to do just that: to demonstrate their willingness to die for their cherished beliefs. The law enforcement officer is prepared daily to put himself into situations which have the potential for serious physical danger to uphold his values.

Also, for most people, their values do not animate their daily lives, or inform their every decision. The law enforcement officer is different. He makes a monumental decision: He swears not just to *die* for those values – although he is prepared to do that, too, if that is necessary – but, even more, he swears to *live* for them. The law enforcement officer chooses a career in which he demonstrates, on a daily basis, that he is willing to *give* his life

– and, even more, to *live* his life – for his deeply cherished values. He models and protects those values every moment he wears that badge.

The goal of any system of spirituality – religious or otherwise – is to infuse a person's life with transcendent value and meaning. Ideally, spirituality teaches that there is no – or should be no – dichotomy between the spiritual ("sacred") and the physical ("mundane" or "profane") parts of one's life. There is no part of life which is – or should be – spiritually neutral. The pursuit of spirituality conflicts with the compartmentalization of a person's life. Rather, spirituality celebrates a life animated in all its activities and aspects by value and meaning, a life that recognizes the significance of one's every thought, word, and action.

However, many people have the "luxury" of compartmentalizing their lives. In their day to day work, they never have to make a decision to fire a gun or put themselves into situations of mortal danger. An accountant, lawyer, dentist, or craftsman might have moral issues that crop up at work, but these moral questions do not rise to the level of life and death, as they do in the work of a law enforcement officer. Even a doctor is never called upon to end the life of a healthy human being.

The law enforcement officer does not have this "luxury" to perform his work in a spiritually-neutral way. The challenges he faces are monumental: each one involves the rights, safety, perhaps the very life of a human being. He finds – indeed, places – himself in the middle of the most unstable, sensitive, and volatile interactions between people. And the consequences of his actions are no less monumental: Life and death – his own and others – depend on his decisions, and he acts as the agent of the law of the United States of America and the instrument of Lady Justice.

With this in mind, it is not an exaggeration to say that law enforcement is perhaps the most spiritual of careers. It demands that the law enforcement officer live, model, and confront daily the noble values to which we all pay lip service from a comfortable distance.

Clearly, the job of law enforcement is laden with deep spiritual significance and meaning. The only question for the law enforcement officer, then, is: Do you recognize the spiritual dimension – and the spiritual greatness – of the activity you are performing?

> Each time a man stands for an ideal, or acts to improve the lot of others, or strikes out against injustice, he sends forth a tiny ripple of hope.
>
> – *Robert F. Kennedy*

Law enforcement is about sending out ripples – more like tidal waves, actually – of hope.

THE SYMBOLISM OF LAW ENFORCEMENT

The law enforcement officer's value as a symbol of hope, as an inspiration to the public he serves, is at least as valuable as any actual law enforcement work he performs.

The department's measure of effectiveness may be the number of arrests the law enforcement officer makes. However, this is not *all* that matters to God; it might not even be primarily *what* matters to God. And, in a very real sense, it's not the way people's souls measure success, either. The world of the spirit measures success very differently: How many people does the officer inspire in the performance of his job? How many acts of kindness, how many times did he rise above the call of duty to provide comfort and concern to uphold a person's dignity?

And that is not meant to minimize the importance of the actual law enforcement work the law enforcement officer does; rather, it is meant to acknowledge the tremendous value of the law enforcement officer as a symbol of all that is noble in the human spirit.

THE CHALLENGES OF LAW ENFORCEMENT
ARE SPIRITUAL IN NATURE

If the law enforcement officer fails to recognize this entire spiritual dimension of himself and his career, then he will be ill-prepared to protect himself against the onslaught to his spirit that the career brings. In such a case, he will have no idea whatsoever about the nature of the forces acting upon him and the challenges confronting him. He will be unable to respond and fortify himself because he will have no real awareness of what is going on. Unclear about the true challenges, he will be looking for solutions in all the wrong places.

His ability to protect and fortify himself and ensure his health begins when he recognizes and acknowledges the intensely spiritual nature of his job.

The next step is to recognize that those stressors that are so integral a part of the job are also primarily spiritual in nature. Every law enforcement officer must confront and negotiate, on a daily basis, in the course of his career, brutal, draining stresses and challenges. These spiritual challenges are unique to, and an inevitable part of, a job in law enforcement.

The law enforcement officer is spiritual, the career and its accomplishments are also spiritual, and so are the challenges to spiritual health presented by that career.

THE KEYS TO SPIRITUAL HEALTH:
AWARENESS AND CLARITY OF MOTIVATION

Obviously, the antidote to spiritual challenges also must be spiritual.

For a law enforcement officer, one antidote to those challenges and stressors lies in his motivation for doing the job. It is the officer's own deeply spiritual motivation that can enable him to successfully negotiate the job stressors and maintain his health. Motivation, it should be noted, is a spiritual concept, in that it belongs completely to the world of the human spirit.

In all likelihood, the officer does not need a new motivation to do his job in order to be able to reap the protective benefits of what he does. But for that motivation to do its job fully and effectively, the law enforcement officer must be aware of it. He need only be aware of the motivation he already has to be able to tap into its protective and restorative powers.

With clarity regarding motivation can come resolve, fortification, strength, inspiration, and health. If he is to have any hope of succeeding in this brutal, challenging environment, a law enforcement officer has to know clearly, consciously, and unequivocally why he does the job. Our ability to help the law enforcement officer, then, lies in our ability to help him recognize the motivation he already has, the motivation that brought him into, and keeps him in, the field – or, if need be, to get a new one.

> One can live in the shadow of an idea and not grasp it.
> – *Elizabeth Bowen*

The law enforcement officer cannot afford to allow his motivation to remain obscure, unclear, or hazy. The stakes of this game are way too high – he dare not allow them to remain shadowy, ungrasped ideas.

There is a profound difference between one who performs the job of law enforcement keenly aware of its – and his own – spiritual nature and one who performs the job oblivious to the true nature of the job – and himself.

Until the law enforcement officer "grasps the idea" and recognizes that noble motivation that pulses within him and brought him to this career, spiritual solutions won't be able to help and fortify him. But once he grasps it, once he recognizes the profundity and spirituality of his own motivation, then he can use it to tap into, and draw freely upon, inexhaustible reservoirs of strength and healing.

There are law enforcement officers who possess these instincts but who are more or less unaware of, or oblivious to, them. Their noble motivations remain half-buried and unarticulated, lost even to the one who possesses them and has sacrificed so much because of them. But if they remain unarticulated, outside of consciousness, the law enforcement officer cannot receive the nourishment he needs in order to continue. He possesses motivation and doesn't even know it. What a sad irony: All of society benefits from his selfless heroic idealism, and he doesn't enjoy the protective benefits.

> One who has a why can survive any how.
> – *Holocaust survivor Victor Frankl,*
> *MAN'S SEARCH FOR MEANING*

A career in law enforcement is fraught with many stressors, temptations, and difficulties. It is hard to imagine how a person could negotiate them all successfully. To this Dr. Frankl answers: If only one has a *why* at the center – a vigorous, robust *why*, one which he recognizes and owns – then he can survive any *how*.

It is fundamentally different to live one's life with a clear sense of purpose and meaning than to live life without one at all, or with a fuzzy one. A person with meaning and purpose can survive – and triumph over – just about anything. However, without that sense of meaning, a person is easily derailed and distracted.

The need for clear, strong motivation in order to survive stressors is not unique to law enforcement or law enforcement officers. But it is particularly relevant for the law enforcement officer because the spiritual challenges of law enforcement are unusually, incomparably intense, harsh, and dangerous. The relationship is proportional: The more arduous, intense and spiritually draining the stressors and challenges, the greater the need for clarity regarding one's motivation.

The intensity of the career of law enforcement is what distinguishes it from all other careers. In less intense careers, you might be able to get by, or even thrive, without consideration of the job's spiritual dimensions; you might not need strong motivation and spiritual introspection to survive. But, in this intensely demanding career of law enforcement, you just don't have that "luxury." To succeed, you have to be motivated and you have to be "in touch with" – aware of – that motivation, the "why," as Victor Frankl calls it. An officer cannot long survive, and certainly never thrive, without that powerful, robust, healthy, meaningful, personal, compelling motivation.

Awareness of motivation carries with it a spiritual benefit in the mystical realm, as well.

Here is a glimpse into the workings of the spiritual realm.

One enjoys a certain measure of Divine protection when he knows that the activity he performs is a fulfillment of a commandment of God. Just knowing that you're fulfilling a commandment of God brings its own protection. Performing that exact same activity ignorant of, and oblivious to, its Divinely commanded nature does not bring with it the same profound spiritual protection.

The activity of law enforcement is an activity ordained and valued by God; in Hebrew, we call such an activity a *mitzvah*. (The word *mitzvah* derives from the word for "commandment" and the word for "connection," because the conscious fulfillment of a commandment of God creates a deep connection between that person and God.)

When a person performs a *mitzvah* unaware of the *mitzvah*-nature of the activity, he derives minimal protection – emotional, spiritual, or psychological – from performing it. However, when that same *mitzvah* is performed with full awareness of its *mitzvah*-nature, the protection one receives is maximized.

For example, a person gives charity to a poor person because it is the right thing to do and he wants to do it. This kind act exists on a certain level. However, when that same person gives charity because God commanded us to take care of the poor, the person creates a connection with God that he didn't have in the first scenario. In the same vein, the performance of law enforcement is a *mitzvah* which can bestow healing and cleansing. That depends upon you and whether you possess the awareness of which we have been speaking. If you "get it," if you're aware of the profoundly spiritual significance of what you do as a law enforcement officer, then you can tap into that potential for healing and cleansing. If you're not aware, you can't.

Recognize that you are a partner with God, do what you do because you are performing the *mitzvah* of law enforcement, and you receive a measure of spiritual protection and fortification. You don't receive as much of this fortification if you remain unaware that you are performing that *mitzvah*.

Attend to the spiritual side of yourself, get in touch with the spiritual motivations that led you into the career. Then, after you are (1) psychologically fortified, and (2) mystically protected, you stand a pretty darn good chance of being able to survive and triumph over anything the job and its stressors throw at you.

WHAT IF YOU ENTERED THE FIELD FOR THE WRONG REASONS?

Individuals enter the field of law enforcement with different motivations and reasons for pursuing a career in law enforcement. Not all of them guarantee success. Clearly, the long-term success of a law enforcement officer's career depends, to an astonishing degree, upon the quality of the motivation the officer possesses:

✦ With strong, clear motivation, the law enforcement officer's chances for success improve dramatically.

✦ Some people are powerfully, meaningfully motivated and have never stopped to think about and recognize this fact. They do not know this consciously about themselves. For them, success depends upon making that which was unclear clear.

✦ With little or no or bad motivation, the law enforcement officer's chances for success are slim. For them, success depends upon their ability to replace that original motivation with a new, worthy one. It can be done. And we can show you how.

IV

FAITH AND SPIRITUALITY

WHETHER they can express it or not, whether they are fully aware of it or not, the fact remains: People who are attracted to the field of law enforcement and who actually become cops are intrinsically very spiritual people. Don't be fooled by that gruff, no-nonsense exterior, or by the characteristic cop's impatience for all that "touchy-feely stuff." In the ways that really count, in the ways that really define what it means to be spiritual, law enforcement officers are as spiritual as they come.

They're spiritual because spirituality is all about being motivated to act and to live one's life according to a set of values that transcend one's own selfish wants and desires. Spirituality is about wanting to have one's life mean something, about wanting to make a difference in the world and in the lives of people. Spirituality involves a recognition that to live selfishly, without concern for other people, is to live a meaningless life.

The law enforcement officer entered a field whose motto and essence is "to protect and serve." It is a field that demands that he spend all his professional life protecting others, enhancing the quality of their lives, and giving of himself. It is a field whose essence is to give: to give unreservedly and fully of oneself, and to give even if it exposes him to danger. Is it possible to find a more altruistic, selfless job? What possible material inducements could be offered that would convince someone to spend his life in this way?

FAITH AND HOPE:
THE COMPONENTS OF SPIRITUALITY

There are two important components to the spiritual yearnings of which we speak: faith and hope. Spiritual people possess faith, and therefore they can hope for a better future.

If those terms, faith and hope, sound too religious, you can use two other terms: confidence and optimism. You can understand faith as a kind of confidence in something, and hope as a kind of optimism in the future. Hope flows from feelings of faith. Where there is faith/confidence, there can be hope/optimism; where there is no faith/confidence, there can be no hope/optimism.

The faith one possesses in one's youth is often a simple, or simplistic, one. It has not been tested or challenged in any meaningful way. It is as naïve as it is idealistic. But it is enough, in the beginning anyway, to motivate one to begin the pursuit of a noble career of service.

Faith can be broken down into three components: faith in God, faith in humanity, and faith in self.

Let us discuss each of the aspects of faith in turn:

1. Faith in God

Faith in God (if an officer has it) runs something like this: God created the universe and, specifically, this planet, and has an active interest in its inhabitants. God endows a spark of Himself, so to speak, that animates every human being with life. He has communicated His expectations for humanity; these include the practice of truth, justice, and kindness. He forbids behaviors that hurt other people. Interested in each and every one of His precious creations, He watches our behavior. Our job in This World is to refine and elevate our souls and characters through performance of worthy deeds and avoidance of misdeeds. Ultimately, in the Next World, the righteous are rewarded and the wicked are punished. There is a process in history: We struggle toward the perfection of This World as we head toward a Messianic era when Evil will be eradicated and Good will prevail.

God governs the world. He has not forsaken or abandoned it; He has not left it to be controlled, or, rather, buffeted, by mere chance and accident. True, He must operate from "behind the scenes," as it were, in order not to destroy freedom of choice that is so essential to our ability to succeed in this world. But hidden in, and operating through nature, He governs His world. God sympathizes, as it were, with righteous people and disapproves of the wicked. He is interested in the lives of people and involved in their growth and development, in that process of refinement of character in which the righteous engage.

If we live properly, in accordance with His dictates for humanity, we are supposed to be rewarded for that behavior, whereas those who disobey God by misbehaving should be punished. It is a logical assumption, predicated upon the principle of "reward and punishment."

As an expression of His interest, God gave us laws by which to govern the interactions of human beings. These laws define decent and moral behavior.

Faith in God translates into faith in the Law. And much of secular law derives its authority, historically and philosophically, from religious law.

Thus, faith in God means faith that He is interested, sympathetic, involved, and present.

2. Faith in Humanity

Every person is endowed by his Creator with a Godly soul. This soul is capable of infinite achievement and greatness. There is essentially no limit to the level of greatness a human can achieve.

We are raised, certainly here in America, to think that people are basically good and decent. Historically, that is the belief that underlies "the American way." So much of our daily experience is filled with images of kindness and decency, of helping another person. Stories dramatized on TV, in the movies, in literature, etc., of heroic, selfless benevolence and altruism reinforce this belief – this faith – in humanity and its goodness. So much of our American culture celebrates the good, decent man or woman. Think Jimmy Stewart or Gary Cooper. This belief has animated our culture since America's beginning. (Despite modern pop culture's single-minded attempt – through its movies, TV, and music – to glorify an immoral, violence-drugs-and-sex-saturated lifestyle that chips away at the notion of the morality and dignity of humankind and replaces it with a grimmer view of humanity, we still manage to cling stubbornly to this notion as a vestige of our long, rich past.)

We live in a society that wrestles with providing for the welfare of all people. Consider advances in medicine, popular debate regarding public policy to achieve equity for all people, to accord all people the blessings of life, liberty. Politicians may debate how to get there, but at the root all are motivated by the same noble aspiration. And all attest to the inherent prevailing decency in humanity as a whole.

Faith in humanity includes faith in the legal system. The laws may be imperfect and incorrect at times, but there is constant effort to correct and further refine the legal system so as to afford the blessings and protection of freedom and safety to every citizen. Indeed, this mechanism that allows for correction and further refinement is one of the most eloquent testaments to the decency and wisdom of the system, a system that expresses the deepest, noblest aspirations of human beings in their attempt to protect and extend the system's rights and blessings to every member of our society.

3. Faith in Self

What one person can do!

Every person who enters a helping profession – and certainly law enforcement is a helping profession – possesses tremendous confidence in his ability to make a meaningful difference in the lives of the people with whom he interacts. The law enforcement officer's career aspirations? They are nothing less than "to protect and serve." Watch the recruit in the classroom, in the gym, on the firing range. What drives him? What's he thinking? He's thinking something like this: "Every thing I learn will translate out there into meaningful action and productivity in my efforts to catch criminals, protect the helpless, ensure order, etc. I am a part – and an important part – of the battle for goodness and justice."

Is there anything great in the world that we don't think we can do when we are young? This youthful confidence may be annoying at times, but it can certainly motivate one to aspire to accomplish big things in the world.

Captain Kirk said it best: "All it takes is one man. Spock, you be that man."

We believe – especially when we are young and enter the field of law enforcement – that we can be "that man."

Making Withdrawals from the Account

Think of the reservoir of faith as a big bank account bursting with resources. The young recruit is bursting with idealism! He is going to make a difference! A person comes into the job with a large amount of altruism, his spiritual capital. He is a rich man in the things that count: faith and hope.

But a person's account of inspiration and goodness can be depleted as constant withdrawals are made. What kind of withdrawals? Every time a person comes into contact with one of the stressors unique and common to, and characteristic of, the job of law enforcement, it drains a little bit of faith, it deposits (as Joseph Wambaugh said) a "daily drop of corrosion on your soul." That's a withdrawal from the account of faith.

That account must be replenished or the reservoir of energy, inspiration, idealism, and passion will dry up. Withdrawals without replenishment lead to spiritual bankruptcy. That is the case of being "spiritually bankrupt," bereft of faith.

A law enforcement officer needs a "drop of healing and cleansing" (McCullough) that can counteract that "drop of corrosion" (Wambaugh) that the work of law enforcement deposits daily on the officer's soul.

Daily, every time a person encounters evil and suffering,

he is withdrawing "big checks" from his spirituality account. If that account isn't replenished in the form of some big spiritual deposits to the account, spiritual bankruptcy results quickly.

The officers who lose that idealism become prime candidates for cynicism, anger, misbehavior, disillusionment, abuse of power, and worse. There is nothing quite as dark or as bitter as the feelings of betrayal that afflict a burned-out law enforcement officer who has lost his youthful idealism.

Take away the engine – the essential beliefs, the dreams and idealism, the very reason for being – that drives a person, and he loses vision, loses idealism, loses motivation. He dies in the most meaningful of ways. His body may be alive physically, but his will is gone, his spirit has shriveled. Such people, though physically alive, are spiritually dead. It is tragic, but not surprising, that such people kill themselves or attempt to anesthetize their pain by engaging in activities that dull awareness.

They are exposed to things that sap and rob them of their idealism. In short order idealism is replaced by anger, cynicism, despair, hopelessness. When there is pain, people anesthetize themselves. When there is no hope, people kill themselves.

There are physical, emotional, and spiritual risks that are the "big checks" presented against the spirituality account. Consider the dangers that characterize a career in law enforcement. The list is by no means exhaustive:

+ Physical danger
+ Shift work, which creates health stresses and exacerbates social isolation
+ The death of a partner
+ Taking a human life
+ Vilification by the public
+ Constant scrutiny by colleagues, supervisors, and the public for mistakes and poor judgment
+ Second-guessing oneself
+ Constant exposure to tragedy, randomness, suffering, and human evil

+ Desensitization, because of constant exposure, to evil, pain, coarseness
+ Loss of faith in the legal system
+ Loneliness and estrangement from family and loved ones because of an inability to share what one experiences (*e.g.*, the gruesome scenes) on the job
+ The need to hide one's feelings and emotions from the general public
+ A sense of impotence

What happens to that account of Faith and Hope after years of presenting big checks without ever making a deposit?

The picture is not pretty. These three deeply cherished values – faith in humanity, faith in God, and faith in self – are assaulted daily in the most brutal ways. Let's look at what happens.

> Whoever fights monsters should see to it
> that in the process he does not become a monster.
> – *Friedrich Nietzsche,* BEYOND GOOD AND EVIL, *Aphorism 146*

FAITH IN HUMANITY

Law enforcement officers see people at their absolute worst.

"Officer safety" requires "hypervigilance" (Gilmartin) – the working assumption that every person may pose a threat, is capable of wickedness and evil. A law enforcement officer develops the attitude that "the brighter the picture, the darker the negative." He must suspect the worst of every person around him. Imagine the damage that wreaks in his faith in humanity!

Ironically, what makes for good (physical) "officer safety" can, and often does, unless kept in tight perspective, make for bad (spiritual) "officer health."

"Officer safety" is a strategy for survival, not a philosophy of life. A person has to be able to check hypervigilance at the door when he goes home at night and replace it with normal caution more appropriate for a civilian.

It's easy to assume the universal wickedness of *all* people and forget that "90% of the people are law abiding and 10% are violators and troubled" (Timboe) when an officer "will deal with this 10%, 90% of the time."

In addition, the failures and flaws of the legal system contribute to a loss of faith in humanity. The bad guys walk as cases are thrown out over minor technicalities and the legal system undermines police work. It's hard to retain faith in the legal system and the human beings who created and maintain it. A law enforcement officer does not need to be reminded that "This is a court of law, young man, not a court of justice." (Justice Oliver Wendell Holmes, Jr.).

FAITH IN GOD

Constant exposure to random, accidental, meaningless tragedy and suffering can inspire the gnawing question, "Who's running the show? How could God allow this?"

The emotional consequences of constant exposure to tragedy are perhaps better understood or more obvious. An officer feels the pain, needs to withdraw, or will be overwhelmed. There is a spiritual toll, as well. Doubts assail the law enforcement officer: Why this tragedy? Did this innocent little child deserve this? It seems so random, this accident. Randomness is contrary to the notion of a God who cares and who directs the world in which we live. God is omniscient, omnipotent, merciful, just; the law enforcement officer sees things every day of his career that seem to refute those beliefs. Randomness and accident, the very meaninglessness of events, all conspire to sorely test and try the belief in Divine Providence.

It is draining to the human spirit to be exposed to seemingly random tragedy.

What exacerbates this problem is that this questioning is going on at a level below conscious thought, without being consciously acknowledged, without the opportunity to air these questions with a colleague or a person of faith, such as a chaplain.

This produces a loss of faith in God. For religious people, the belief that God governs the world in ways that human beings cannot comprehend provides a measure of comfort. However, this is a concept that must be constantly reinforced.

FAITH IN SELF

The law enforcement officer watches as all the relationships in his life – the key ones – wither and die. The officer watches helplessly the process of estrangement from his family and loved ones. He wonders where the anger and the antipathy come from. He never felt them before, he doesn't understand the harshness with which he responds to his family's questions, the shortness and impatience that characterizes his interactions with them. There is in all of this the feeling that one is acting out a script written long ago, that one is helpless to change the inevitable unhappy ending.

Dr. Gilmartin, in his book *Emotional Survival for Law Enforcement*, identifies one of the long-term effects of overidentifying with one's police role to the exclusion of all other roles, with putting all of one's emotional and psychological "eggs" in the one "basket" of "I'm a cop": Officers develop an attitude of victim-based thinking. Such victim-based thinking produces some bizarre attitudes and behavior. It accounts for the transformation of an officer's "core values" (absolute, objective moral values) into "situational values" (relative, subjective pseudo-moral values). Often, this victim-based thinking inspires a sense of "entitlement" which allows an officer to engage in the "luxury" of behavior that, once upon a time, he would never have considered, would have rejected outright.

A spiritually healthy law enforcement officer enforces the law fairly, professionally, and dispassionately. On the other hand, a spiritually unhealthy law enforcement officer abuses the law, enforcing it arbitrarily, even cruelly.

This does not go unnoticed by the law enforcement officer himself. He watches himself bend or break laws he once revered, laws he promised to uphold and enforce. Even if he is not aware of the steps that got him to this point, he is nevertheless aware of this transformation in himself – and he is not proud of it. He might engage in the behavior, driven by forces that Dr. Gilmartin identifies, and he might rationalize it to those around him. But he is left with the vague and disquieting feeling that he has betrayed something that was once very precious to him. His soul watches as he betrays the ideals he once cherished and protected. On a level below conscious thought, perhaps, the officer is ashamed of his corruption and abuse of power, and he feels loss of faith in himself.

The angry veteran looks at himself in the mirror and wonders: What happened to that idealistic young law enforcement officer who entered the field not so long ago with such high hopes, with idealistic dreams of "serving and protecting," aspirations of fighting for "truth, justice, and the American way"? He sees that angry, frustrated, bitter, cynical, estranged, lonely rule-breaking veteran. By all measures that he once had, he has failed. He has failed as a family man, he violated and betrayed the law and his own inner set of core values. Indeed, by what standard can he be considered anything other than a failure?

℘℘℘

Never having replenished one's faith in God, humanity, or self, and never having made spiritual deposits into the spiritual account, the law enforcement officer goes into spiritual overdraft and, finally, spiritual bankruptcy. The law enforcement officer hits bottom, exhausted, dispirited, feeling betrayed, adrift without anything to believe in. Where once the world and future were bright, there is only darkness. If there is no hope, what is the point in continuing? What potential is there for things to improve? What ability is there to make a difference? The future holds no promise of ever getting better. The pain is unbearable. He will do anything to remove or numb the pain – either temporarily (in all the forms of self-medication) or permanently (in the form of suicide).

The law enforcement officer suffering in this way must recognize that he is not alone. What he is experiencing – the anger, the disillusionment, the sense of betrayal, the cynicism, the disappointment with himself – is very common, whether his fellow officers will admit it or not.

It doesn't have to be that way.

It is possible to retain one's idealism even in the face of unbelievable provocation, if one makes regular spiritual deposits to that account within one's soul.

That's the challenge of using spiritual tools to support and bolster a career in law enforcement.

An officer needs a regular, sustained way to reinvigorate and replenish the reserves of spiritual energy.

The next chapter will discuss practical, effective ways to replenish the spiritual account, to preempt spiritual overdraft and bankruptcy, to promote faith and hope.

Help is on the way!

V

TOOLS FOR RENEWAL

SPIRITUAL STRATEGIES
FOR REINVIGORATION AND RESTORATION

THE big question, of course, is: *Is it possible to replenish that supply of idealism and inspiration? Is it possible to restore Faith and Hope?*

In this chapter we will present strategies for renewal and reinvigoration.

Over time, the faith that will be replenished will, in all likelihood, not be that youthful, naïve, simplistic kind the officer had at the beginning of his career. In the wise officer, youthful, immature faith grows into mature, even profound, faith. This constantly replenished faith, tempered by the officer's many years of experience and exposure to people and events (which the civilian never sees or dreams about), will be more complex, but more powerful. It is a faith tempered in the fires of difficulty and challenge. It is a faith that has confronted the worst life and humanity can dish out and it has prevailed.

The goal, of course, is not to restore youthful, naïve idealism. You've seen and been through too much to recover that youthful naïveté. You wouldn't even want to have that perspective back, because it's just not true. It's not your destiny, it seems, to possess naïve views of the world. A better goal is to replace the cynicism and hopelessness and despair that took the place of youthful naïve idealism with mature, wisdom-filled idealism and with belief in the same values with which you came into the job. They were pretty good ones, and they have changed, shaped, and molded the world over the millennia in the face of some daunting opponents.

It may be worth noting that none of these tools are meant

to promote one particular type or brand of idealism. There's no universal, abstract "idealism," a "one size fits all." Each officer needs to pinpoint his own unique, highly personalized brand of inspiration. It's not that he has lost his idealism and now needs an infusion of new idealism from without. I'm not offering you an inspiration transfusion, the same way one would receive a transfusion of someone else's blood. Far from it. Instead, my goal is to nurture the idealism that is buried in you, still there, where it's always been and never left you. You need merely affirm it and let it shine brightly again. The difficulties of your experiences have blocked up your natural wellspring of spiritual strength and inspiration. I can help you to unplug it so it can flow freely again. I only need to put you in touch with that inexhaustible reservoir of faith and hope that resides within every human soul, upon which you have drawn in earlier times, and which motivated you to pursue this career.

A law enforcement officer has the greatest likelihood of success, and the greatest protection from spiritual stressors, if he (1) has got the right kind of motivation, and (2) is clearly aware of, and in touch with, that motivation.

What tools help?

The depletion takes place on three levels, so the restoration must address each of these components, as well. There must be deposits in the form of restoring:

+ faith in God
+ faith in humanity
+ faith in self

Not surprisingly, a tool may support more than one area.

Strengthen these faiths, and you increase the chance for survival and success.

SPIRITUAL TOOLS FOR SPIRITUAL SURVIVAL

Many of these exercises are best done with a journal. You

might need some time and some space and some privacy. And you definitely need some honesty and a sense of humor. Some can be done alone; some, with a group. When working with a group, there is only one rule: No one ridicules. If it's a group you want, find a group of guys whom you can trust: The role peers can play – those colleagues and other people who share your idealism – is enormous. Group members can record their thoughts and answers anonymously, then toss them into the center; the writings can then be read aloud for all to discuss.

Not all tools can be used every day. Some can be used frequently; others, infrequently. That's OK. Have as many tools in your repertoire as you can.

1. Perform a self-exam regularly.

Any good doctor will tell you about the importance of frequent self-exams for early warning signs of disease.

The next time you're standing in front of the mirror checking for bumps and lumps and dark spots, don't forget to check your attitude. Does it also have dark spots on it? Do you find yourself becoming increasingly cynical and disillusioned? Is everyone in the world a criminal or a pervert?

Be aware of the warning signs that indicate spiritual danger.

Just as we would consult with a doctor if we found signs of physical illness, we should be vigilant to address any early warning signs of spiritual dysfunction.

If you found a lump on your body, you'd consult a doctor. If you find a blemish on your soul, consult a doctor of the spirit – *i.e.*, a chaplain.

2. Identify your own source of inspiration.

Idealism is like a fingerprint: Each one is unique. What is your style? Where does it come from?

a. Is it religious, or does it come from some other philosophy?

b. What or who first inspired you to become a law enforcement officer?

c. How did you first become aware of this inspiration?

3. *Visualize a person who inspires you.*
Have a conversation in your mind with him/her.

Did s/he ever encounter setbacks or frustrations? What effect did it have on that person?

Tell that person, "All I've done, and try to do, is because of your example."

What does s/he say to you?

Allow yourself to be inspired again.

Return to your youth, if only for a moment. Who inspired you? Was it Batman or your Uncle Frank? The Lone Ranger or Mother Theresa? Or maybe your Aunt Theresa, the one who worked vice for LAPD for years? Zorro? Inspector Harry Callahan? Encyclopedia Brown? All in their own ways fight the good fight for justice and decency. (One exception: If it was Miami Vice, forget it – you're doomed.)

Reduce them to their fundamentals. What's different about them from you? What's the same? The mask and the cape are meaningless – they're just outer trappings. (But, for heaven's sake, put away those white suits and lavender T-shirts.) At the heart of the matter, what's the same?

4. *Consider the following questions:*

+ What careers other than law enforcement did you consider?
+ What are the three most important benefits you derive from being a law enforcement officer?
+ What are the three most significant sacrifices you make?
+ How does this compare to other career choices you might have made?

✦ How many members of your family are in law enforcement? How many members of your family are in the clergy?

✦ What does a minister do? What does a law enforcement officer do?

5. Meditate.

Construct a prayer or meditation – not a formal one, but in your own words. Or use one that already exists and means something to you. In either case, it should be something that has the ability to inspire and focus you.

For example, it could be your agency's mission statement. Every agency has its own mission statement. Study yours carefully. Reread it. Use it as a text for quiet, sustained meditation.

The purpose of revisiting a prayer or meditation over and over again is to remind yourself of fundamental truths and values you possess, the ones that can get lost in the course of a hectic life.

What does your prayer or meditation say? What does it say to you?

If you'd like, use a picture or an object to meditate on and allow it to inspire and calm you.

Here is a sample prayer:

> Master of the Universe, grant me the strength and wisdom to enforce the laws of the United States of America with fairness and justice. Let me perform my duties not for ego or self-aggrandizement, but for Your sake and for the sake of Your children. Allow me to be the instrument through which You demonstrate Your concern and mercy to Your creatures. Keep me, my partners, and my family physically safe, emotionally sound, and spiritually healthy. Accept my frustration and pain as a sacrifice I offer to you, and grant me comfort and relief from the wounds – physical,

emotional, and spiritual – I have received. I thank You for giving me the opportunity and privilege to work on Your behalf, as Your partner in the creation and perfection of Your world.

6. Seek out the services of a good chaplain.

Law enforcement officers can derive tremendous comfort from interacting with clergy.

The clergyman is an invaluable resource because he spends much of his life thinking about, and dealing with, the world of the human spirit. He spends his time with the ideas of nobility, idealism, justice, and compassion without cynicism and without sneering. The good clergyman can recognize, appreciate, honor, and encourage the noble exercise of the spirit even when that noble spirit is trying, from modesty or lack of awareness, to masquerade as something mundane. A clergyman is like a living Geiger counter that can detect spirituality buried beneath layers and layers of modesty, pain, sarcasm, or bravado.

You don't have to be members of the same religious system to get something out of a good chaplain.

A chaplain shouldn't be trying to convince you of something new, foreign, unfamiliar, or counterintuitive *to you*. A chaplain shouldn't be trying to convince you of something you don't already know and live.

A good chaplain provides comfort and strength because he holds up a spiritual mirror so that the officer can see who and what he really is, so that the law enforcement officer can identify and own the essential spirituality at his core, the spirituality that motivated him to become, and that motivates him to remain, a law enforcement officer.

The mirror a chaplain holds up is like one of those magical mirrors in a fairy tale: It shows you what you really look like underneath it all; it shows you your true self. And your true self resembles a minister. The magical mirror has a hard time telling you two apart – you are both people of faith and idealism, devoted to helping people.

A chaplain looks at a law enforcement officer and sees a priest – a high priest – of love, compassion, self-sacrifice, justice, responsibility. A good chaplain holds up a mirror so you can see that, too.

7. Go to church/synagogue/mosque.

Express your frustration or bewilderment. Pray. Ask for comfort or clarity or strength.

You have earned the right to make your opinions and requests heard. After all, you take care of His children.

And it's OK if you express anger or uncertainty. Spirituality is a relationship between you and some higher power. All relationships have their ups and downs.

And listen, too. You might pick up an insight or two.

Take Steve McGarrett's advice: "Book 'im, Danno." It's not a bad idea. Spend some time with a good book – *the* Good Book, in fact. Reacquaint yourself with the source of your – and our society's – deeply cherished spiritual and moral values.

8. Use the precious gift of fellow officers well.

Peers can be an invaluable resource for many reasons. Don't squander them.

Interaction with fellow officers can be extremely helpful and therapeutic.

Who better than a fellow officer can understand the unique stressors, problems, and grinds that confront an officer daily in the performance of his law enforcement duties? If a fellow officer is willing to admit – and not all will – that he, too, wrestles with these same spiritual problems, the knowledge that other officers experience the same thing can itself be very therapeutic. Acknowledging that such feelings are normal dispels the dangerous, illusory notion for an officer that he is alone in feeling this way. For a cop trapped in the diseased macho mindset that cops must be invincible and admit no pain or weakness, the mistaken notion that one is alone in suffering this way can be an incredibly lonely, debilitating feeling. Such an officer will mistakenly perceive himself as being "weak" compared to other "strong" cops – which is probably the worst indictment for a cop trained to revere strength and present an image of invincibility to the world, his superiors, and himself.

In addition, in the best case, officers can acknowledge and encourage the best in each other. Look at your comrades in arms. You might be able to see the greatness within them, the nobility of spirit, the commitment to transcendent truths and values that you fail to see in yourself. Know that they see it in you.

Beware, though! In the worst case, officers can reinforce each other's bitterness and cynicism and infect each other with toxic spiritual germs. If you recognize this tendency in some of your peers, stay far away.

9. Focus on the inherent goodness in other people.

Recognize the strategic value of – and inherent danger in – practicing excellent "officer safety." It will keep you alive physically, but it may kill your soul spiritually.

Recognize that "officer safety" is a strategy for survival; it is not a philosophy or a worldview. It is not based on certainty, only on a suspicion. What works well in the field and has great operational value may rob you of one of the best resources you might ever have: your faith in human beings.

Recognize the decency of other people. You don't need to replace the selfishness, immaturity, evil, or criminality you encounter in the course of your day with perfect, absolute righteousness – although there are some people who have come pretty darn close. You just need to see decency, a desire to be good and do good, an instinct to improve. You're not perfectly righteous yourself, but you're one of the good guys. You need to see some other non-police good guys. They're out there.

Visit a soup kitchen, a hospice, or an old age home where

volunteers help people every day. Find other arenas where goodness is the main thing.

Your goal as a spiritual human being is to learn to bounce between these two states – one a necessity on the job, one a necessity off the job. With time and practice, you *can* get better – though perhaps never perfect – at bouncing between these two states.

10. Reframe the accident scene.

Every cop has 'em: memories. And you can't seem to shake 'em ... ever. Memories of the gruesome crime or accident scenes. They come back at night in dreams or when you're driving down a rainy road.

Replay the scene (you can't help it), but this time pan out. Pull the camera back. Get a picture of the larger scene. Use a wide-angle lens. You're missing some important clues. Realize that this larger scene encompasses some elements you might not have picked up on: you and your colleagues. If there is evidence of human callousness and wickedness at this accident or crime scene, there is also evidence of much human decency and concern. The emergency personnel, the EMTs fighting to resuscitate that victim or the dignity of the body, the firefighters battling the blaze, the police processing the scene – these institutions and individuals exist to affirm the sanctity of life, to protect the dignity of every human being, to ensure that justice is served and to dissuade those who would do this again.

You might have missed it, but the rest of us didn't. We can't consider the scene without including you in our picture. You remind us that not all people are evil, not all people don't care. You remind us that some people even put themselves out, inconvenience and endanger themselves, for our sakes and for the sake of principles and institutions and people we hold dear. We couldn't survive even our brief, superficial, rubbernecking-delay exposure to the accident scene if you weren't there. Because you were there, our nightmares are less intense, our fear is counterbalanced by confidence and hope.

Replay the scene, if you must, but replay *all* of it, to be fair.

The complete picture also encompasses the number of near accidents that don't turn out to be catastrophic, the victims who do survive, and the fact that these are still the aberrations of life. God is protecting us and keeping us safe. It's the unusual situation that ends in disaster.

11. Don't confuse who you are with what you do.

You entered the field because you wanted to help people. That's your job description as a human being. You help people not because you are a cop; you help them – and you are a cop – because you are a human being.

There's a great episode of "Early Edition" in which we learn that Gary Hobson was chosen to receive "tomorrow's newspaper today" because, in his youth, long before he was given the supernatural help of "the paper," he was actively helping the people around him. Thus, he was deemed worthy to receive this instrument capable of helping countless people. The paper doesn't make him what or who he is. He chose a path for himself, made himself what he is, a long time ago, without the help of props and gadgets. The paper only supplements that. So, too, your badge and gun and squad car. They enhance what you can do; they don't define who you are – you did that a long time ago … and continue to do that every single day of your life.

Your commitment to those noblest human values does not end when your shift ends. It's *not* about your job; it's about who and what you are. You champion those exact same values in all the roles you play in your life, albeit in different ways. There is always the danger of overidentifying as a cop to the exclusion of all other roles. You're *not* "just a cop"; you are a model of responsible kindness everywhere you go, in every role you play.

Help someone in your role as a human being, in your guise as a civilian, as a private citizen. Don't make a citizen's arrest. Instead, carry in the old man's groceries. Volunteer occasionally in a soup kitchen. Not because you heard there is shady stuff going on in the back, but because you want to remind yourself that, even before you pledged to serve and protect as a cop, you yearned to help as a human being.

12.
Find a way to measure
your practical and spiritual effectiveness and value,
other than by the traditional one
of "number of arrests made."

How about number of people helped or inspired?
To that end, identify your "starfish."

A story is told about a little boy walking by the shore. He made his way gingerly along the beach, being careful to avoid the thousands of starfish washed up on the shore. He noticed a man in the distance who was busily throwing starfish back into the water.

The boy approached the man. "What are you doing?" he asked.

Without stopping his work, the man replied, "Just what it looks like – I'm throwing the starfish back into the water before they die."

"But don't you realize that you'll never be able to throw them all back in?" the boy asked incredulously. "There are thousands of them!"

"Does it matter that I can't save them all? I saved this one, and this one, and this one, and this one ..."

Keep a diary, a daily account of your benevolent acts and the people you have helped. Total up your account on a monthly and yearly basis to keep track of how you're *really* doing.

We're not advocating that you set goals too low. Rather, recognize, and enjoy, each individual act for what it is: a stunning victory. Every tour of duty has at least one, probably many.

True, there are lots of starfish still out there, yet to be touched by you. You'll get to them. For the moment, though, think about the ones you helped today. There will be plenty of time to think about those other ones later. Just for right now, find your starfish for today.

13. Stop a criminal career – before it starts.

Cops are reactive. As far as that goes, it works. But what if *you* could be proactive and stop crime even before it starts? Inspire someone to walk the straight and narrow path by your actions in law enforcement.

Plant some seeds for the future. It might require a little effort, but the rewards can be tremendous. You don't need to know what will happen after you plant them. Rather than sitting around and waiting for criminals to develop, you've planted seeds.

In your uniform, smile at a child, a child who might not hear the most favorable things about cops while he's growing up. He'll never forget the memory of your smile. Because, to him, it's not your smile; it's a smile from a cop, it's a smile from the legal system of the United States of America, of Lady Justice. You've put a human face, human warmth, compassion, respect onto the legal system you represent. Maybe the law, maybe authority need not be inhuman and inhumane in their eyes. Or offer an encouraging word. You'd be amazed at how much bad press you can counter. Who knows what fruit that will reap in the future? You might have ended or preempted a criminal career before it ever started.

How many movies involve traveling back through time to change history? What if you could travel back through time and dissuade someone from walking that twisted path? Well, guess what? You're back there right now. Do it now.

In This World, you'll probably never know what your efforts accomplished. In the Next World, you will.

14. *Maintain your values and integrity.*

I know a community that introduced a simple exercise called "WWBD" to its police department – that is, "What would Batman do?"

Sounds stupid? It isn't. It actually contains a bit of profundity to it. Allow me to speculate and explain the logic behind this apparently silly exercise.

Ever had the experience of trying to maintain your position in the water at the beach? You think you've succeeded ... until you happen to notice the multicolored beach umbrella that used to be opposite your position on the shore is now far down shore. Turns out that while you were talking in the water, thinking that you hadn't moved at all, you had drifted far, far away from your original position.

It happens to all of us in our lives.

Because of constant exposure to emotionally and morally corrosive individuals and situations, cops can slide from possessing absolute values and standards of morality to relativistic ones (*e.g.*, "Compared to them – [and that "them" can be pretty slimy, when you consider the unsavory characters cops encounter] – I'm a saint"). It can be disastrous – morally, professionally, personally – for a law enforcement officer.

How does one maintain a constant, inviolate value system in the face of an onslaught of rationalization, immorality, temptation, and situational moral relativity? Isn't it inevitable that the corrosion will change you?

Is it logical to assume that, just because an officer came into the career with a well-developed value-system, he will be able to maintain it in the face of all the challenges the career presents? Isn't such moral and ethical deterioration inevitable?

The cure: A daily position check from the GPS of absolute standards and values of morality. Daily synchronizing against something fixed and unchanging can play the same role as that multicolored umbrella on the beach: You can use it to correct your position and prevent yourself from drifting *way* downstream on the river of moral relativism.

Compare to something that also constantly shifts and you can lose yourself big-time. You need to be able to check in and check against something which is fixed and unchanging.

"WWBD" is an exercise that forces an officer to compare his instincts and behavior to the gold standard of an idealized, perfect, mythical law enforcement officer. How would such a law enforcement officer, free from temptation, laziness, callousness, graft, and personal self-interest, behave in this situation? How are *you* behaving in this situation?

Maybe you've floated downstream. Maybe you paddled vigorously to get there. Maybe it's time to correct your position.

"WWBD?" Silly? Perhaps. Light-hearted? Definitely. Stupid? Definitely not.

Don't like "WWBD"? No problem. Use "WWIE*D," instead.

15. Relinquish control back to where it belongs: with a Higher Power.

Don't succumb to a sense of hopeless resignation; rather, give over control to that which is beyond you.

Have a clear sense of division of labor. It's not your job to right the world, to perfect it, to eradicate all evil, to ensure the final triumph of justice in the world. That is God's job, and He will do it. Every one of us has his own specific job description and we should concern ourselves with doing that, not with doing God's job. Keep yourself on the team of the good guys.

You are like a doctor fighting to save a patient. Ultimately, there is only so much a doctor can do, and then it is up to God to decide whether He will send healing and health. Doctors also struggle with letting go of control after they have done everything possible.

You work with God, but you don't have final control over the outcome. He does.

---

* Inspector Erskine.

What do you have control over? The way you conduct yourself in your struggle on behalf of good – that's your ultimate victory, one that introduces untold spiritual energies into the world and ennobles it.

16. Bask in your successes.

Even the Batman – cold, emotionless, driven champion of justice, avenger of evil – has a Trophy Room in the Batcave. As driven and single-minded as he is, he too needs to be reminded once in a while of his past successes. It keeps him going.

You need your own Trophy Room. Keep a journal of your accomplishments on a daily basis. Record even small successes. Furnish your Trophy Room carefully. Stock it thoughtfully. Walk through it (mentally) periodically.

Let's review briefly what constitutes a "success" and what you should put in your mental Trophy Room.

All law enforcement officers have their "glory shots": the pictures of those mega-busts and mega-hauls.

What are *your* glory shots? More importantly: what's *next* to them? Pictures of family and loved ones. Pictures of non-police accomplishments.

Your Trophy Room should have a healthy mix of tributes to professional successes, pictures of trips and time with family and friends, and memorabilia that remind you of youthful times and idealism – not just pictures of guns and cocaine.

17. Find internal motivation.

Anyone in law enforcement has had the outrageous, maddening experience of listening as a good, decent cop gets taken over the coals by the media. They don't know the realities of law enforcement work, the split-second decision-making it requires, the pressures. And so they prattle on and on, and withhold the respect that the law enforcement community deserves.

This illustrates an important principle: the need for internal motivation.

There is a fundamental difference between one who performs the job of law enforcement "internally directed" and one who performs the same job "externally oriented."

When one does what one does from a place of inner clarity of purpose, from an internally defined sense of purpose, the career has much to offer in the way of satisfaction and development of character. The work will be nourishing and fulfilling, and it will contribute to a further refinement of character, in accordance with the psychological principle that "We are made kind by being kind" (Hoffer). For one acting from within, each act of kindness inspires an additional, deeper attitude of kindness.

But what about officers who feel decidedly *less* kind after doing the job? What's going on with them?

If one performs the work of law enforcement in need of approval, acknowledgement, accolades, or external affirmation from the outside world, then he's doomed to disappointment, frustration, and rage. If one measures his self-worth by the outside world, if one needs the approval of others, then the career holds nothing but disappointment.

You have to do the job from a place of strength, from an internally directed value system. The starry-eyed approval or knee-jerk disapproval of the public doesn't mean anything to you. Its presence or absence will affect nothing. In that case, your job can ennoble you; it will be nourishing and fulfilling.

But if you are doing this for the external affirmation, because you need the world's approval, then you are bound for disappointment – and worse. The reporters' barbs will rankle and torture you. They have way too much power over you because you have given them that power. They have something you want, and you can be sure that they are going to withhold it. In fact, they couldn't give you enough honor. For the person who is hollow inside, who has no inner sense of self-worth, there is no amount of honor the outside world can give that will truly satisfy him for very long. He's like a drug addict, always in need of the next fix. Recognition becomes stale very fast and the "approval junkie" constantly needs a new supply. Consider the stars in Hollywood who just can't get enough attention and fanfare. Like them, the "approval junkie" is doomed to eternal frustration.

In this case, each act of kindness you perform in the course of your duties will not nourish or ennoble you; on the contrary: because you're choking back all that disappointment, frustration, resentment, and rage, it will only bring you down, make you bitter because of your insatiable need for affirmation from an unaccommodating world, which cannot, in any event, supply you with what you really need.

Perform kindness from a place of strength and you will grow great; perform that same kindness from a place of weakness and you will grow bitter.

Do one thing – quietly, anonymously – every day to remind you why you do what you do: because your spiritual value system inspires you to. Don't let any other motivation dilute the performance of this act of decency or kindness. Perform your duties, filled with respect for yourself, not needing the approval, gratitude, or accolades of the public you serve. Know that you remain true to yourself, to your value system, to God. Enjoy how that feels. Enjoy His approval – ultimately, the only approval you really need.

18. Recognize that you are a symbol.

Is it a coincidence that most TV shows since the beginning of TV have been police shows? There were years that all prime-time programming was about policemen and detectives. Is that mere coincidence? Think again.

You are a symbol to every clear-thinking citizen of this country. You are a rallying point, a symbol of hope against the chaos that threatens civilization and would engulf it in a moment if you were not there. As you were inspired, so too you inspire others who will take up the mantle – as cops or people – after you have retired, or will practice decency and heroism in their private civilian lives.

Imagine: You are about to talk to that impressionable young person who turns to you with wide eyes. What do you have to say to him? Was it all just meaningless? Impossible! Distill your experiences into some wisdom. Share some wisdom with him.

Kojak used to ask, "Who loves ya, baby?" The answer, of course, is God: He loves you for tending to and protecting His children.

19. Choose your symbol and symbolism.

"Hey, who was that masked man? ... He left this silver bullet." What a profound exercise in humility. Did he need admiration or gratitude? Not one bit. He did it for one reason: to remain true to the highest-minded values he had, the values to which he had pledged undying loyalty.

A silver bullet is a symbol of immutable integrity and steadfast loyalty to the principle of justice.

What does your bullet stand for? What's it made of?

20. Confront the pain.

Don't disown the pain. Recognize and embrace it for what it is: the clearest proof of, and a tribute to, your humanity and compassion and nobility of spirit. The pain is, well, painful, but the wish ought not to be that it go away completely. That pain is a profound expression of your humanity. If you can witness evil or tragedy without being affected or sickened, you shouldn't be doing this job. The one who should be fighting evil is the one who least wants to fight, who doesn't relish the fighting at all. Confronting and fighting evil, taking a human life, is painful. But the goal is not to be desensitized until one doesn't care or feel that pain anymore. That pain is an expression of your deep regard for the sanctity of human life. That pain should communicate to you that the agency, indeed, chose well when it gave you a badge and a gun and the authority to enforce its laws and protect your fellow citizens. Woe to us all on the day when one who is incapable of feeling that pain puts on the badge.

21. Take your oath.

Oaths are symbolic acts, and symbols are spiritual in nature. Oaths possess a spiritual, transcendent quality to them, directing our thoughts away from the world of the concrete and material to the world of the spirit, to the world of ideas.

When I was a kid and read comic books, I used to get a thrill every time Hal Jordan would recharge his power ring to become the Green Lantern: "In brightest day, in blackest night, no evil shall escape my sight. Let those who worship evil's might beware my power: Green Lantern's light!"

Do you have an oath? How often do you say it? At the beginning of your career, at your graduation from the academy? Not often enough.

Many decades later, I still remember that fateful scene in which Batman administered the oath to Dick Grayson before he could become Robin. Dick Grayson's hand was on the Bible, and Batman instructed him: "Swear by all that is holy that you will never deviate from the path of justice."

Construct your own oath. Say it daily.

The unromantic types call it a mission statement. What are your core values? Write the mission statement of your law enforcement career. You don't have one, you say? You just go with the flow, wherever it carries you, with no clearly stated defined goals? You're in serious danger.

Write your mission statement. Laminate it. Read it every morning. Then turn into Green Lantern.

22. Remind yourself: You're doing a mitzvah.

As we explained earlier, a *mitzvah* is an activity ordained and valued by God; the Hebrew word "*mitzvah*" connotes the ideas of "commandment" and "connection," because the conscious fulfillment of a commandment given by God creates a deep connection between that person and God. Knowing you're doing a *mitzvah* brings spiritual protection. You enjoy a certain measure of Divine protection when you perform – consciously, purposefully – the Almighty's commandment. Perform that exact same activity oblivious to its Divinely-commanded nature and you miss out on that protection.

Perform your job consciously, purposefully, and proudly, completely aware of its rich dimension of spirituality, and you'll reap a wealth of protection, physical, emotional, and spiritual.

23. Be proud of your scars.

People who work and sacrifice for the well-being of others are sometimes brought down or contaminated. No law enforcement officer, exposed to the sadnesses of the career, ever escapes totally the hardening, contamination, or jading of the profession. Naïveté and simple beliefs in humanity are not the province of the seasoned law enforcement officer. No law enforcement officer ever escapes completely unscathed the coarsening of language or etiquette.

Don't revel in the process, but don't beat yourself up over it, either. Recognize it for what it is: a sacrifice offered freely by the law enforcement officer on behalf of others. That's the way that God understands and considers it.

24.
Do something nice for yourself (without spending a fortune).
Remind yourself that you are someone pretty important.

It is worth repeating Eric Hoffer's insight that we quoted earlier, in chapter 1: "[W]e really do love others as ourselves."

Our ability to empathize and look benevolently at the rest of the world depends upon how much empathy and benevolence we demonstrate for ourselves. If we neglect ourselves and allow ourselves to languish unattended, we will not be able to feel concern for others – and that's why we entered this career in the first place.

You have to love and care for yourself in order to do your job properly. The care and feeding of *you* is the indispensable prerequisite for you to be able to function effectively – compassionately and empathetically – as a law enforcement officer.

You took an oath to "protect and serve." It is a strange tragic irony that the one citizen out there in your world who does not enjoy the benefit of your protection and service is you.

Do something to "protect and serve" *yourself* – you, who are our finest resource.

VI

THE ROLE OF A GOOD CHAPLAIN

A note to chaplains (with law enforcement officers listening in):

It's probably worth reviewing quickly what exactly a good chaplain does and, more importantly, does not do. Many studies and interviews, and much anecdotal evidence, suggest that many chaplains have failed their constituency by trying to proselytize, and not all members of the clergy are suited to be law enforcement chaplains.

First, let's get straight what your job description is *not*:

It's not to proselytize. And it's not to undermine the legal system or create conflicts of loyalty.

Not all clergy are capable of this kind of restraint – only the secure ones are.

Too many chaplains do both those things – especially proselytize, as they try to see how much they can "get away with." They don't comfort at all; on the contrary, they cause more conflict and pain.

What, then, is the real job description?

1. Support the spiritual well-being
of the law enforcement officer
with whose care the Almighty has entrusted you.

You don't have to know everything about every religious system, as some chaplains mistakenly think. Your job is no different if you deal with a member of your faith or with a person who belongs to a different faith tradition or, perhaps, to none at all.

You have to know something about the human spirit and its longing to make the world a better place. You have to recognize within the law enforcement officer his nobility of spirit. You have to be able to acknowledge it and give honor to it, all the while avoiding empty flattery and pat answers about anything.

2. Talk a little, but listen much more.

A good, competent chaplain can accomplish some pretty amazing things, often without uttering a single word! We call this ability to comfort without uttering a word a "ministry of presence."

3. Remind the officer that there are people who take the world of the spirit seriously.

4. Acknowledge that you see in the officer a fellow high priest – a person for whom the world of the spirit is significant.

A good chaplain holds up a "magic mirror" so that the law enforcement officer can recognize the innate spirituality within himself. It is a profound contribution to an officer's well-being, because this new-found self-awareness has the ability to nourish, protect, strengthen, and rejuvenate his flagging spirits.

5. The "sigh" of a chaplain is comforting.

A good chaplain reminds you that high priests – of the law or the Law – don't have all the answers. Why is his sigh so much more significant than anyone else's? In essence, it says, "I, who am identified as a champion of faith, don't have all the answers, either, but I continue the fight – just as you do." It is honest and humble; it gives you permission not to understand.

A chaplain can comfort because he doesn't have all the answers, but he still fights the good fight. Many grim, tragic, wicked things happen that the chaplain cannot explain; he's at a loss as to why God did what He did. But that doesn't derail him or rob him of his faith. Sometimes not having the answer is devastating: An officer might feel that, unless he has the answers, he can't continue, he can't believe, he can't hold onto faith and hope for the future. It's not true.

The greatest gift a chaplain can give is his honest confession, his open admission, that he "just plain doesn't get it" sometimes. He doesn't understand why God allowed what He did to happen. His admission of total confusion ... and pain, even as he refuses to give up and throw in the towel. What a gift! What a comfort!

Sometimes all this can be communicated without saying a word!

6. Help to influence the shape of the meaning that a law enforcement officer attaches to events.

Events and interactions with other people can be understood and interpreted in different ways. People don't always say what they mean or mean what they say. Conversations and exchanges can be vague and inconclusive. And an officer can easily fall into the trap of "awfulizing" experiences.

Listen to the officer's story, of course, but don't accept unquestioningly his "take" on what happened. Don't interrogate or cross-examine him, but do try to get a global picture and a larger perspective. Then, gently suggest a different perspective that one could adopt in understanding and evaluating the events the officer described. Often it is the spin we attach to an essentially neutral event that charges that event with positive or negative energy, meaning and significance.

7. Teach about control.

A big challenge for law enforcement officers is control and the lack of it.

In debriefing, we try to give them back a sense of control (*e.g.*, "Would you like water or orange juice?").

Sometimes, when officers interact with a chaplain, they can

feel that they have little or no control, especially if the chaplain is bludgeoning them with his religious perspective of things and giving him pat answers. This will only heighten their sense of frustration and of being "out of control," making them feel even worse and making the problem even more acute.

In your conversations with officers, let them have control, let them set the tone.

> **8. It goes without saying, but it needs to be said: Never be a snitch, acting on behalf of the agency to discover information for them.**

∑ℛ

A good chaplain is a lot like the Lone Ranger: At the end of every TV episode, the grateful townsfolk would ask, bewildered, "Who was that masked man? We never even got his name." You've done your job well if, at the end of your encounter with an officer, he, too, can wonder, gratefully, "Who was that chaplain?" That is: who was he religiously? What religion did he represent? "I never even got his name (*i.e.*, religion)." That's the ultimate indicator of a chaplain's success.

(You might wear distinctive clothing that identifies your religious affiliation, but pretend the officer closed his eyes.)

VII

CONCLUSION

A COMPLETE, INTEGRATED CONCEPTION OF "OFFICER SAFETY"

OFFICER health doesn't just happen by itself; an officer has to work at it. In fact, given the nature – the particular hazards – of the job, an officer has to work *hard* at it. Achieving *complete* officer health requires an overall regimen designed to protect and fortify body, emotions, and spirit.

New technologies and ongoing research continue to provide new, improved equipment and protocols. We are getting better at ensuring the physical safety of officers. Statistics show that the number of officers who die at the hand of another person has decreased significantly over the last several decades.

But the numbers of officers who, because of job-inspired stress, drink, self medicate, cheat, divorce, or die by their own hand have not come down; they stay stubbornly consistent and way too high. We can and must work together to bring those numbers down; it's not going to happen on its own, and we don't have the luxury of ignoring all those casualties. Those officers are victims – emotional and spiritual victims – of the job, a job that is emotionally and spiritually draining.

Ensuring the *emotional* health of officers (*e.g.*, enabling them to both pursue their careers and still maintain a rich non-officer dimension of their lives) is important. But officers will always be vulnerable to job-inspired stress – and they will express that stress in the form of substance abuse, domestic disharmony, even suicide – if they do not attend to their *spiritual* health, as well.

For a law enforcement officer, the spiritual dimension is

not just *one more* dimension of the job. For the true, really conscientious, officer, it is the *central* dimension, it is *the* very reason he went into the career. Most officers, whether they know it or not, entered the field inspired by a spiritual desire. There can be no more spiritual a desire than the desire "to protect and serve."

For some officers, the more self-aware ones who recognize the importance the spiritual dimension plays in their lives, it might be easy and natural for them to attend to it. They know clearly why they do this job, and so they can draw freely on that deep reservoir of spiritual strength and idealism that exists within every human being, and they can replenish that spiritual reservoir frequently. They know how to replenish their supply of faith and hope so that they never run dry or feel that they are spiritually overdrawn. For every "drop of corrosion," they know they must, and they know they can, and they know how to, generate a "drop of cleansing and healing."

For others, this does not come easily. They may not even be aware of the spiritual dimension of the job, or of the spiritual stirrings that motivated them to take the job. Or perhaps they vaguely sense it. That's not good enough. Those officers are vulnerable; they are at risk. And, all too often, they succumb. Those are the officers lurking behind the distressing, heart-breaking statistics.

Essential for sustained *total* well-being is *spiritual* well-being, and, for the law enforcement officer, that means having a strong sense of *why* he does the job.

The law enforcement officer least suited for the long term is one who enters the field with weak, meaningless, or non-existent motivation. If it's all about power, glory, and macho posturing, then that officer doesn't have a good chance for long-term success. Those cowboys, the John Waynes of the bunch, are in serious danger of succumbing to every symptom we've described. For even they, even late in the game, with rare exception, can turn it around and replace lousy or anemic motivation with good, healthy motivation.

An Officer Needs a Full Arsenal
of Tools, Resources, and Techniques
to Keep Himself Completely Safe.
What's in that Arsenal?

✦ For physical safety, his arsenal includes: training and review in physical exercise and combat, the importance of waiting for backup, use of handcuffs, use of force, the nonverbal messages their actions and behavior send, traffic stops, off-duty performance, and searches.

✦ For emotional health, his arsenal includes: training and review in the need and ability to maintain a diversity of roles beyond the cop role, the importance of aerobic exercise to combat the effects of the "hypervigilance behavioral rollercoaster" (Gilmartin), aggressive time management, post critical incident debriefing, and peer support.

✦ For spiritual health, his arsenal includes: training and review in connecting with the original sources of his inspiration and motivation, resources for renewal and on-going infusions of inspiration and motivation and clarity, tools for understanding his professional aspirations as a cop within the larger context of a noble, idealistic desire to do good in this world, opportunities to recognize and reaffirm the practical, symbolic, and mystical role of law enforcement, opportunities for reminding oneself that there are good, idealistic people in the world (the other "90%," with whom the officer rarely interacts [Timboe]), resources for restoring faith in God, faith in humanity, and faith in oneself, tools for finding opportunities to express the noble aspiration to "protect and serve" to enhance one's sense of wholeness and integration.

Thus equipped, an officer has an excellent chance of having a long, healthy, successful career.

Every law enforcement officer, even the healthiest and most idealistic, at one time or another becomes dispirited in the course of his career. The career exposes the law enforcement officer to intense things – he just can't escape it. He wonders about the justice of that value system he supports and his place in it. He wonders about the inhumanity of humanity. He wonders about the apparent ungodly behavior of God. He questions himself, his worth, and his choice of such a stressful, painful, demanding career. He flounders and he thrashes around. It is a very painful ordeal.

For the officer who has never explored this dimension of himself and his reasons for entering the field, this can be devastating, even life-threatening. At that point, when he is already out in the field and in the middle of a crisis, it is hard to get back on track, to regain one's focus. That is clearly not the optimal time to first learn about the spiritual component of law enforcement, to explore one's motivation for doing law enforcement, and to begin recognizing and nourishing one's spiritual side.

Care should not begin post-crisis. It must begin pre-crisis, in the academy, *long before* an officer will ever need to tap into, and draw heavily upon, his spiritual reserves. Spiritual survival should be part of the academy training. Those who design academy curricula and oversee training academies must incorporate this into the standard curriculum and teach officers to devote time to this long before the problem exists.

"We Need Better Spiritual Coping Skills. We Need to Be Healthier Going In, So We Have a Chance of Being Healthy Coming Out."

An officer with a ready reservoir of spiritual strength – one who recognizes and "owns" his "*why*," has explored his motivations, has stockpiled resources in his spiritual reserves – will respond in a fundamentally different way to the crisis than one who has no comparable source of strength.

Conventional wisdom has it that all law enforcement officers "hit a wall" five years into their careers; this can happen as early as one year into a career in law enforcement.

The severity of the crisis, the degree of the disillusionment, the self-destructive behaviors engaged in – all, or most, of these can be preempted, or, at least, minimized, if there is serious preparation in advance.

Amazing, isn't it? The whole process – including what an officer does, why he does it, the stressors of the job, the solutions to those stressors – is deeply spiritual. That might have been surprising to hear once upon a time, before reading this book, but it certainly shouldn't be now.

You don't have to – nor should you – be the *victim* of a career in law enforcement. There's no reason to stagger out of a career in law enforcement as a bitter, cynical, angry, burned-out husk of a human being. Some law enforcement officers retire from successful law enforcement careers with their families and relationships strong and loving, their integrity intact, their consciences clear, their idealism undiminished, their souls untarnished, their reputations sterling, their gaze bright and clear and benevolent, their language G-rated, their faith and hope radiant. They look back with pride over their long careers, happy and satisfied that they made a difference in many people's lives. With pride in their work and satisfaction in the destiny they chose for themselves, they turned the mantle over to the next generation, confident that there are others who will continue the fight on behalf of Good and against Evil. They enjoy knowing also that their good work in the career does not end when they hang up their shield. Through their personal example, they continue to inspire the next generation to take up the battle, emulate their high level of professionalism and idealism, and try to make whatever difference one law enforcement officer can make – which, by the way, is plenty.

To know that one creates and leaves a legacy of kindness and concern, and inspires another generation – what more can a person have hoped for from a career or from a life?

One deeply spiritual law enforcement officer expressed himself thus: "Anyone who does this work sees it. Death. Their own. Their partner's. People they care about. Death is with you the entire time. But we go to work anyway because, ultimately, even death itself is powerless against you if you leave a legacy of good behind. Even death itself is powerless against you if you do your job well. ..."

You can use the information contained in this book to avoid spiritual illness. But even more, you can use it to pursue spiritual health and vitality.

Your career in law enforcement can be rewarding, and can leave you fulfilled, not bitter; caring, not isolated; idealistic, not disillusioned.

Insights into spirituality and spiritual survival like the ones described in this book were not available for earlier genera-tions as a standard feature of every academy curriculum. Those officers who did not know about spiritual survival suffered as a result of their lack of awareness. But they're available now, for all to use. Take advantage of them.

If you have seen the worst that humanity is capable of sinking to, you have also seen the best that they are capable of climbing to. It's worth noting that, in many cases, and for many people, that "best that they are capable of climbing to" is *you* – what you do and what you stand for. "Liberty and justice for all," regardless of race, creed, color; ensuring the rule of law, ensuring the safety of the weak from the strong, enabling people to pursue their destinies free and unmolested. What a glorious expression of the human spirit, this concept of universal justice. You dedicate your life to protecting those kinds of noble concepts and making them work in a free society.

If your career introduced you to the depths of depravity that people can sink to when they exercise their free will to choose evil, your career also introduced you to the heights of nobility that people can rise to when they exercise their free will to choose good. If you cannot see it within yourself, see it in your colleagues, other officers, and first responders with whom you have worked – and know that they see it in you.

When you revise your sense of self, and recognize the essential spirituality at the core of what you do, then many kinds of irresponsible and destructive and self-destructive behaviors are seen for what they truly are: unworthy of you.

The manner in which you enforce the law is at least as important as the particular laws that you are enforcing.

Said one seasoned officer, "Perform your duties *passionately*, but not *personally*."

A spiritually and emotionally healthy law enforcement officer enforces the law properly and dispassionately – *i.e.*, firmly, but not cruelly. Professionalism in the performance of the job is an extremely accurate indicator of the spiritual and emotional health of an officer. A healthy officer does not interpret violation of the law as a personal affront to him. The officer is the priest of that law – but it is not *his* law. He stands for something much bigger than himself and his own ego; there is nothing personal in his enforcement of the law.

One of the most powerful indications that an officer has a healthy spirituality about his job is his ability to enforce the law dispassionately. For the healthy officer, it's not about ego. It's not a personal contest of machismo between him and the law-breakers out there.

It might seem counterintuitive and ironic, but it's real: *If a law enforcement officer is passionate about his commitment to protect and serve, if he is spiritually aware and at peace, then he enforces the law dispassionately* – *i.e.*, objectively, fairly, consistently.

Conversely, if the officer is not at peace, is spiritually unhealthy, then every law-breaker's violation of the law becomes an affront to the officer, a challenge, a personal insult. That might seem to make for good law enforcement – officers passionate about the law, "taking it personally." In fact, it is anything but good law enforcement; it paves the way for abuse, racism, and violent, arbitrary and inconsistent enforcement of the law.

In contrast, consider the officer who is at peace, with nothing to prove, secure in the inviolate, transcendent truth and supremacy of that law. That security allows the officer to enforce the law dispassionately. Dispassionate enforcement of the law is the greatest tribute to, and indicator of, the spiritual health of the officer and, by extension, of the system.

Spiritual health will flow through the officer outward to all of society. As each individual officer goes, so goes the community and, by extension, society. The stakes are that high!

There are things a law enforcement officer learns in the academy that make for good street survival. But when these same things are applied outside the context for which they were intended, they can make for destructive life attitudes. An excellent example is the tactic that lies at the heart of "street survival": Hypervigilance demands that an officer anticipate danger from every person, and requires that he see every person as a potential threat. Once the shift ends, "spiritual survival" requires something completely different: that an officer anticipate, and provide for the possibility of, the potential greatness that every person possesses.

It is not easy to bounce between two states – one (on the job) that translates practically into profound mistrust of human nature and one (off the job) that views people so much more sympathetically. And you have to learn to do it in a way that will not slow you down on the job, or deprive you of an attitude that is crucial for survival on the job and one that is crucial for survival off the job.

The act of reminding oneself occasionally that the tactic is "act as if" and not "act because" – that the tactic is based on a suspicion and not on a certainty – is beneficial. What are the alternatives? To accept it wholly and unequivocally? That way brings its own dangers. Remember the suicide statistics: More officers die by their own hand than by others' – on average, about three times as many. To accept this tactic as life philosophy doesn't ensure officer safety. Rather, faced with loss of hope and faith in humanity, officers often kill themselves.

Another excellent example is the way an officer relates to the concept of control. "Never surrender to anyone or anything" is a good on-duty philosophy for an officer. Off-duty survival requires relinquishing control to where and Whom it belongs.

You have shown your willingness to die for a lofty ideal. Choose now to live for that ideal. You can accomplish much more that way, for yourself and for others, off duty and on. This book will help you do that.

Just because we discussed the problem doesn't mean it's going to go away, of course. It's clearly not. The job remains stressful. That next crime or accident scene is still going to be gut-wrenching. We don't want to desensitize you to the pain or the challenge contained in that crime or accident scene. Indeed, that pain you feel in response to encountering suffering or evil is convincing proof that you're the right man or woman for the job. I'm not saying that the questions and the stressors don't exist. And I'm not saying that there are simple answers to these questions – or, at times, that there are any answers at all. But to see another side, a larger picture, to better understand the role you play, the impact you have, the team you're a part of … can give you hope and allow you to continue to give it to others.

We chaplains represent many different religious traditions and there is much that distinguishes our personal beliefs. But there is much that we share in common. For each of us, as for each of you, the world of the spirit animates everything that we do.

And we do not always have the answer.

We are sometimes troubled, bewildered, saddened, angered by the evil, injustice, sadness, tragedy, suffering that we see. We look defiantly up at heaven or gnash our teeth in impotent rage and fury. We are sometimes wracked by doubts. Our faith in humanity, God, and human institutions such as the legal system are sometimes sorely tested.

But then we return to work. Because there is work that needs to be done in this world, to fix it and ourselves.

Love of God is troubled love, sometimes beset by doubt and questions. But doubts pass, or they don't, and a deeper love sets in in its wake.

One need not be ashamed that one wrestles with faith.

If I have not provided answers, I have, at least, I hope, provided a framework for addressing the questions.

Acknowledgments

Many people contributed to the creation of this book, and it is my pleasure to thank them publicly.

A special thanks to Dr. Stephen Band, Chief of the legendary Behavioral Science Unit of the FBI, and SSA Sam Feemster for introducing me to the need to provide spiritual fortification for law enforcement officers. Sam's observation that "In the academy we teach how to do the job; we also need to teach why to do the job" was an important motivator for me in doing this work. Because of my association with the BSU, I have been privileged to meet, observe, speak with, and interview hundreds of fine law enforcement officers. Steve and Sam, your devotion to both the letter and spirit of the law is an inspiration to me!

Sgt. Craig Hungler and Father Michael McCullough are first-rate professionals, top-notch colleagues, and wonderful friends. Since we first met at that FBITN satcast long ago, they have inspired me by their single-minded concern for the well-being of all law enforcement officers.

In my thinking and the development of my ideas, I have been greatly influenced by the work and writings of Dr. Kevin Gilmartin. This book and many of my ideas about spiritual survival are built logically upon ideas he presents in his excellent *Emotional Survival for Law Enforcement*. You will find many parallels between phenomena he describes in the emotional world and what I describe occurring in the world of the human spirit.

A special note of gratitude to Sherry Horowitz for all her hard work on the cover and Adam Simms for editing and typesetting.

It would be impossible to properly thank my wife Marsha for even one of the roles she plays in my life. She is my inspiration, my collaborator, my critic, my editor, my friend, and the love of my life.

My motivation for writing this book was to repay the law enforcement community and its officers in some small way for the services they provide and for the blessings they bestow upon each and every one of us living in this glorious country of ours. My parents, Edward and Esia Friedman, have spent a lifetime sensitizing me to recognize these blessings. This book is a monument to their patriotism and wonderful sense of gratitude.

CAF
Linden, N.J.

BIBLIOGRAPHY

Coupe, Sandra Lee, ed. *Selected Readings for the Next Millennium: An Anthology of Recent Publications by the FBI Behavioral Science Unit (BSU) 1996-1999.* Washington D.C.: U.S. Department of Justice, 1999.

Gilmartin, Kevin. *Emotional Survival for Law Enforcement.* Tucson, AZ: ES Press, 2002.

Pliskin, Zelig. *Gateway to Happiness.* Brooklyn, NY.: Aish HaTorah Publications, 1983.

Sheehan, Donald C. and Warren, Janet I., eds. *Suicide and Law Enforcement: A compilation of papers submitted to the Suicide and Law Enforcement Conference, FBI Academy, Quantico, Virginia, September 1999.* Washington D.C.: U.S. Department of Justice, 2001.

Twerski, Abraham J. *Twerski on Spirituality.* Brooklyn, NY: Shaar Press, 1998.

About the Author

Rabbi Cary A. Friedman is the Rabbi of Congregation Anshe Chesed in Linden, N.J.

He received an MSEE from Columbia University and Rabbinic ordination from Yeshiva University.

Rabbi Friedman was a Chaplain at Duke University and Executive Director of the Jewish Learning Experience of Durham, N.C., and a Chaplain at the Federal Corrections Institute in Butner, N.C.

He is a consultant to the Behavioral Science Unit (BSU) of the FBI. He is the author of five books (including *Table for Two*, *Marital Intimacy*, and *Wisdom from the Batcave*) and numerous articles.

Rabbi Friedman is married with six children.

Compass Books

Additional copies of *Spiritual Survival for Law Enforcement* are available from **Compass Books**. Mail in this order form with payment or contact us by e-mail or through our website to receive one or more copies. *(Quantity discounts are available upon request.)*

Shipping and Handling

Please add to the total price $5.00 for the first book, and $1.00 for each additional book. Add $6.00 for the first book, and $1.50 for each additional book for priority delivery or delivery to Canada.

We also accept orders by e-mail (please be sure to include the information requested in the order blank below):

E-mail: SSLE@spiritualsurvivalbook.com
Or visit our website: www.spiritualsurvivalbook.com

Order Form

I would like _____ copies of **Spiritual Survival for Law Enforcement** @ $19.95 each.

NAME _____

ADDRESS _____

CITY _____ State ___ Zip _____

TELEPHONE _____

Payment
(Please do not send cash.)

❏ Check or money order payable to "Compass Books" is enclosed
❏ Please charge my ❏ Visa or ❏ Mastercard

Account #: _____ Exp. Date: _____

Signature _____

Send payment with this order blank to:

Compass Books
Dept. SSLE
P.O. Box 3091
Linden, NJ 07036

Compass Books

Additional copies of *Spiritual Survival for Law Enforcement* are available from **Compass Books**. Mail in this order form with payment or contact us by e-mail or through our website to receive one or more copies. *(Quantity discounts are available upon request.)*

Shipping and Handling

Please add to the total price $5.00 for the first book, and $1.00 for each additional book. Add $6.00 for the first book, and $1.50 for each additional book for priority delivery or delivery to Canada.

We also accept orders by e-mail (please be sure to include the information requested in the order blank below):

E-mail: SSLE@spiritualsurvivalbook.com
Or visit our website: www.spiritualsurvivalbook.com

Order Form

I would like _____ copies of *Spiritual Survival for Law Enforcement* @ $19.95 each.

Name _____

Address _____

City _____ State ___ Zip _____

Telephone _____

Payment
(Please do not send cash.)

❏ Check or money order payable to "Compass Books" is enclosed
❏ Please charge my ❏ Visa or ❏ Mastercard

Account #: _____ Exp. Date: _____

Signature _____

Send payment with this order blank to:

Compass Books
Dept. SSLE
P.O. Box 3091
Linden, NJ 07036